Prima's Official Strategy Guide

David S.J. Hodgson

 SO-AHM-606

Prima Games

A Division of Random House, Inc.

3000 Lava Ridge Court
Roseville, CA 95661
(916) 787-7000
www.primagames.com

Product Manager: Jennifer Crotteau
Project Editor: Michelle Trujillo

Contents

Acknowledgements

The Author would like to thank everyone on the *007 Agent Under Fire* team including Stephen Blankenship, Jon Horsley, and Jason Vanderberghe; extra special thanks to Philip Campbell and Jason Delong for their sterling efforts in the deadline maelstrom; Scott Blackwood, Marcel Laforce and all at EA Canada; Electronic Arts all Staff; MGM all Staff; Gary Harrod, Richard Leadbetter

007 Training

Ah, there you are, 007. We'd like to give you some idea of the perils that await you, and before you jet off to save the world, it might be a good idea to brush up on your skills and take a look at this training document we've prepared. We've gathered the following information to make your missions go as smoothly as possible. Good luck!

Controls

It will take a little time to become familiar with the various Bond controls. However, the default control scheme is the easiest for most players, though experts may decide one of the other schemes is superior.

There are three types of control setups in this game. One is for the action portions, where you'll be on foot, generally equipped with weapons and gadgets. Then there are the driving portions of the game, where you control the latest in vehicular technology. Finally, there are "rail-shooting" stages where you are in a vehicle, but not driving, allowing you to concentrate solely on the mission at hand.

Perfect the three types of control (the game manual has all the details of each type) to obtain the best possible score. Your country depends on you!

Difficulty Settings

There are three difficulty levels for single-player games: Operative, Agent, and OO Agent. The points awarded after each mission affect which secret characters, levels, vehicles, and other rewards are issued. Real agents play the game on the most difficult setting, where guards react faster, and damage you receive is just a little more severe. At the OO Agent level, you won't be able to rely on your sophisticated auto-aim capability any more. Make a mistake on the higher levels of difficulty, and it might be your last!

Modes of Play

James Bond enjoys a single-player challenge as much as the next man, but he's also encouraged to take on foes in specially created combat zones. Thankfully, this game doesn't disappoint—you can play in Single-Player or Multiplayer mode. Check out the multiplayer chapter later in this guide.

Secret Agent Maneuvers

By now, you should have learned basic control moves, such as walking forward, aiming, reloading your weapons, and how to cycle through your Q-Gadgets. But you'll also need some expert moves to complete the game unscathed. Here's how to make the most of your control pad.

Sidestepping (or Strafing)

Once you have mastered moving forward, backward, and turning, try strafing. Press ⬜ to sidestep left, and ⬜ to sidestep right. This is an excellent way to avoid enemy fire.

Circle-Strafing

The most complex of Bond's maneuvers, this involves moving in a circular pattern around a position (usually a foe you are firing at). Start by pressing ⬜. As you start to move to the right, press and hold ⬅. You should now be moving in a counterclockwise circle. Now adjust your view so that the enemy you are strafing around always appears in the targeting reticle in the middle of the screen. That way, you can continue firing as you circle him.

Attacking Airborne Foes

At first, you may have trouble attacking airborne targets. Going after helicopters is simply a matter of looking up (⬜) to target them. The problem comes when you move around a level while targeting an enemy without looking at the ground. Keep targeting the enemy, pausing to flick your view down to check that you're not stuck against scenery or walls, then look back up and continue to attack.

Close-Range and Long-Range Combat

The "Inventory, Armory, and Vehicles" section of this guide details the weapons best suited for close-range and long-range combat—essential knowledge for joining any combat scenario. The Shotgun, for example, is an excellent weapon from a few feet away, but it's useless at range. Conversely, the Sniper Rifle is excellent at long range, but terrible in a close-range firefight. Use this information when selecting a weapon.

Decreasing a Guard's Accuracy

Finally, you can greatly decrease the chances of being hit by crouching, lateral movement (such as strafing), and by quickly moving out of the guard's line of sight. This only works temporarily until the guard begins to close in, or you move into view. Conversely, you can make yourself more vulnerable to a guard (and increase their accuracy) by standing still or in an open area, or allowing guards to target you.

Exploding Barrels

You'll find numerous orange and red barrels throughout the environment. You can target enemies within range simply by firing at the barrels. The barrels explode after a couple of shots, taking out any nearby foes. The wooden crates eventually explode, but without the force of a barrel, and shooting the compressed-gas canisters on the forklifts create an impressive explosion. Don't stand near these barrels yourself—you're just as susceptible to splash damage as the enemies are!

Splash Damage

Splash damage is damage caused on the peripheries of an area-of-effect weapon, such as a Rocket Launcher. These weapons cause large explosions. Don't fire them near walls, or you'll receive some of the damage. Use projectile weapons that cause splash damage (such as Grenades and Rockets) in open areas to minimize the chances of being hit by your own weapon.

The Bond Points System

Bond, you'll find that you will be intensely scrutinized on your missions, and much information will be recorded for the experts back at MI6. When you complete a mission, you'll be judged on how competently you handled yourself in seven different categories. If you reach a certain points total, you will receive special rewards.

Points System Example

The following table illustrates examples of minimums and maximums for each element of the level completed, and the associated scores. These results are shown on the mission results screen, and do not appear if you abort or do not complete the level.

Score Categories

Bond Moves

Each mission has a set number of Bond Moves that the player can make. Each action is worth a set number of points, and the Results screen indicates how many actions are possible in the mission, and how many you performed. For specific information on the moves, consult the mission walkthroughs.

Enemies Subdued

This displays how many adversaries are in the mission, and how many you've taken down. The target value is static; guards that run in after initial firefights do not count toward the target value.

Special Modifier: Hand-to-Hand Bonus

Agents who use hand-to-hand combat techniques rather than ordnance will receive two times (2X) the score for each adversary subdued. The use of non-lethal force is often necessary to achieve maximum score.

Ammo Efficiency

This is a percentage value, calculated as kills/shots. The points given to the player is calculated as the player's scored percentage of the possible number of points for the category.

Weapon Accuracy

This is a percentage value, calculated as hits/shots fired. The points given to the player is calculated as the player's scored percentage of the possible number of points for the category.

Damage Taken

This is a percentage value, calculated as the damage the player has taken/damage target, which is determined per mission.

Mission Duration

This is the time the player takes to complete the mission (not counting cutscenes), with a time target. The player is scored against the target number; completing the game within this time limit results in full points. The more time you take past the goal (up to a maximum time limit), the lower your points awarded.

007 Bonus

Number of 007 Bonus Pick-ups the player recovered during play in relation to the total number of Bonus Pick-Ups on the map. You receive the 50,000-point bonus *only* if you collect all the Pick-ups. You must already have a Gold Medal to collect these items.

Points System Example

Category	Expert	Novice	Maximum Points
Bond Moves	7 out of 7	0 out of 7	20,000
Enemies Subdued	45 out of 45	0 out of 45	20,000
(Remember, agents who use hand-to-hand combat will double their points!)			
Ammo Efficiency	100%	5%	15,000
Weapon Accuracy	100%	5%	20,000
Damage Taken	0%	100%	15,000
Mission Duration	1:53 out of 2:00	4:53 out of 2:00	10,000
007 Bonus	7 out of 7	0 out of 7	50,000
Total	–	–	150,000 (100,000 plus 007 Bonus)

Special Modifier: Difficulty Multiplier

Your final score varies depending on difficulty level. The difficulty multiplier is applied after all of the scores are totaled. Guards are tougher, better shots, and cause more damage the more difficult the level.

Difficulty	Multiplier
Operative	X1
Agent	X1.5
00 Agent	X2

Medal System

Providing you score enough points, you are rewarded with one medal per mission; your current medal is displayed in the Mission Select screen for each mission. There are four medals, ranked from easiest to hardest to receive. Note that Platinum Medals are only available once Gold has been achieved. Generally, play the game on Operative to receive Bronze Medals, Agent to receive Silver Medals, and 00 Agent to receive Gold Medals—although you *can* earn higher denomination medals at lower levels if you play skillfully.

The Bonus Scoring System

Defeating the evil of Identicon's global empire isn't the only plan of action, 007, as there are a number of additional surprises awaiting the secret agent with enough skill and aplomb to score highly in each mission. The exact nature of the rewards on offer is strictly confidential, but the following tables indicate just what you have to do to earn perfect points during your sorties. Remember to multiply the scores by 1.5 or 2 to find the totals for Agent and 00 Agent difficulty levels.

Bond Moves Mission Data

The following tables show what you need to do to complete the mission and earn extra points, become efficient and accurate with ammunition, finish quickly and with full armor, and take out all enemies. Each Bond Moves factor is then added together for a mark out of 20,000.

Mission 1: Trouble in Paradise

Factor	Points Awarded
Q-Claw to top of entrance	2.000
Use Q-Decryptor on door 1	3.000
Use Q-Decryptor on door 2	2.000
Open armory door	5.000
Q-Laser gate to glass walkway	2.000
Blow up fork lift	4.000
Drop crate on enemy	2.000
Total Moves	7

Mission 2: Precious Cargo

Factor	Points Awarded
Blowing up the Gas Station	2.000
Using the gas barrels to take out the foot soldiers in the plaza	1.500
Using the gas barrels to take out the foot soldiers by the generator in factory	1.500
Dropping the gunner out of the first helicopter	1.000
Dropping the gunner out of the gas station helicopter	2.000
Taking out the tires on the various pursuing vehicles (x6)	1.500
Taking out both foot soldiers with rockets at the end of the central corridor in the factory	1.500
Taking out the two foot soldiers on the gantry to your left by shooting the explosives between them	1.500
Total Moves	13

Mission 3: Dangerous Pursuit

Factor	Points Awarded
Using Q-Smoke on an enemy vehicle	4.000
Getting the armored van with your first Q-Pulse	4.000
Take out the roadblock at the dock by shooting the gas barrels to the left	4.000
Take out some foot soldiers at the dock exit by shooting the barrel on the ground	4.000
Take out several foot soldiers posted near the convention center gas station by blowing up the station	4.000
Total Moves	5

Mission 4: Bad Diplomacy

Factor	Points Awarded
Destroy Sentry Laser 1	3,000
Destroy Sentry Laser 2 (Use your Q-Specs to locate the control panels for the sentry lasers.)	3,000
Access Secret Room (Second Floor)	2,000
Q-Claw to Second Floor	2,000
Retrieve Keycard	3,000
Retrieve Griffin's Passcard	4,000
Destroy Sentry Laser 3	3,000
Total Moves	**7**

Mission 5: Cold Reception

Factor	Points Awarded
Retrieve Computer card	3,000
Entering first ductway	2,000
Photographing the oil rig model	3,000
Using Computer Card to silence alarms	4,000
Q-Clawing up to duct in caves	2,000
First time downing a foe using steam cistern	2,000
Retrieving first Q-Remote program	2,000
Opening first Q-Remote door	2,000
Total Moves	**8**

Mission 6: Night of the Jackal

Factor	Points Awarded
Retrieving Sniper Rifle from Balcony	2,000
Q-Clawing to MI6 safe house	2,000
Q-Clawing to Embassy	2,000
Freeing hostages	4,000
Opening secret flag door	2,000
Rescuing Damescu	2,000
Pushing Carla into fan	2,000
Defeating helicopter with Sniper Rifle	4,000
Total Moves	**8**

Mission 7: Streets of Bucharest

Factor	Points Awarded
First Section	
Using the Q-Slick on a pursuing vehicle (1st time only)	2,000
Two-wheel maneuver after Data Chip	2,000
Jumping the Blown Bridge	2,000
Making first Rooftop Shortcut jump	2,000
Downing both Helicopters in the train station	2,000
Second Section	
Hit Gas Barrels in Courtyard causing chain reaction	2,500
Downing the helicopter after courtyard	2,500
Hit gas barrels beside limousine during Q-Vision section	2,500
Dispatching the helicopter above the bridge	2,500
Total Moves	**9**

Mission 8: Fire & Water

Factor	Points Awarded
Retrieve Q-Remote crane program	1,000
Q-Remote crane on first helipad deck	2,000
Q-Laser door lock	1,000
Q-Laser duct 1	2,000
Q-Laser duct 2	2,000
Q-Remote lower crane 1	1,000
Q-Remote lower crane 2	1,000
Snipe helicopter 1	2,000
Q-Claw to catwalk in pump room	1,000
Q-Claw to second large cistern	1,000
Q-Remote crane on tower deck	2,000
Snipe helicopter 2	2,000
Q-Claw to top tower cage	1,000
Total Moves	**13**

Mission 9: Forbidden Depths

Factor	Points Awarded
Shooting the red switch at the first security station	3,000
Shutting off both steam valves	6,000
Destroying all three vertical fans	6,000
Shooting the red barrel in Warehouse	5,000
Total Moves	**4**

Mission 10: Poseidon

Factor	Points Awarded
Q-Laser first hatch	2,000
Retrieve Q-Remote program 1 (Lab 1)	2,000
Retrieve Q-Remote program 2 (Lab 1)	2,000
Retrieve Q-Remote program 3 (Lab 1)	2,000
Turn on lasers before guards are alerted in Lab 2	2,000
Set Q-Remote target 1 (Lab 2)	2,000
Set Q-Remote target 2 (Lab 2)	2,000
Set Q-Remote target 3 (Lab 2)	2,000
Lower bridge (sub bay)	2,000
Total Moves	**10**

Mission 11: Mediterranean Crisis

Factor	Points Awarded
Q-Claw Keys	500
Get in vent from Zoe's cell	1,000
Q-Laser open chainlink gate	1,000
Q-Claw stealth route 1	1,000
Q-Claw stealth route 2	1,000
Retrieve Harrier Q-Remote program	1,000
Use Harrier program to defeat guards	2,000
Q-Claw to conference room	1,000
Snipe helicopter	3,000
Q-Laser Missile technician's bonds	2,000
Retrieve missile Q-Remote program	1,000
Q-Slide	1,000
Activate Zoe's crane (before she is free)	2,000
Q-Remote missile	2,000
Total Moves	**14**

Mission 12: Evil Summit

Factor	Points Awarded
Q-Laser weapon case	2,000
Retrieve Q-Remote program in tower	2,000
Q-Remote door in walkway	1,000
Q-Slide from Tower 2 to Tower 1	2,000
Q-Slide from Tower 1 to Control room	2,000
Shoot cable (drop console)	4,000
Rescue hostage in silo 1	2,000
Rescue hostage in silo 2	2,000
Rescue hostage in silo 3	2,000
Rescue hostage in silo 4	2,000
Total Moves	**11**

Going for Gold

The Gold Target score is displayed on the Mission Select screen. After you receive the Gold Medal, the Platinum Medal target is displayed on the Mission Select screen instead of the Gold Medal target.

If you score enough points, a Medal Reward screen follows the scoring screen that congratulates you on your success, displays the medal you received, and lists any other bonuses that this medal unlocks. The early missions have lower thresholds for medals than later missions.

Platinum Medals are unlocked by scoring enough points for a Gold Medal, and collecting all 007 Bonus Pick-ups in the mission. This is indicated "+ 007" appearing after the "Target Score" field in the Mission Select screen.

Special Item: 007 Bonus Pick-Ups

007 Bonus Pick-ups are spinning, floating 007 logos that appear in each mission if and only if you have previously earned a gold medal for that mission. Upon replaying the mission after earning the gold medal, you will find that there are 007 Bonus Pick-ups scattered throughout the missions (3-9 Pick-ups per mission). The pick-ups are placed off the beaten path, and you will need to know the level very well to find them all.

Training Complete

Well done, 007! I hope you're ready to face the danger ahead. Be a good chap and familiarize yourself with the following cast of friends and foes, and then come to grips with your weapons and Q-Gadgets.

Characters

Allies

In the world of secret-agent espionage, enemies are numerous. Utilizing the personnel from the British Ministry of Defense is paramount to your success in the combat zone. With this in mind, we present the people you'll be liaising with during your numerous missions.

M

Your mission commander from MI6, M is a stickler for detail. Her mission briefings tell you everything you need to know.

Objectives may change during a mission. At any time, you can read the current objectives on the Pause screen. M's importance to you cannot be overstated.

CLASSIFIED: IMAGE NOT AVAILABLE

R

A master inventor who has served for years in Q-Branch under the watchful eye of Q, R delivers the gadgets you need. Some of his projects have taken years to complete, and he gets a bit testy when they are misused or destroyed. If R appears during a mission, listen carefully to what he says.

Zoe Nightshade

One of the CIA's undercover agents, Zoe Nightshade will help you stop Adrian Malprave. Expect to rendezvous with her in Hong Kong, where Adrian Malprave's organization has an offshore facility. Zoe is skilled with a variety of firearms, and is a world-class driver. You'll be best off handing her the keys, 007, while you concentrate on thwarting the enemy. Nightshade is a valuable and highly important agent, so treat her accordingly.

Doctor Natalya Damescu

Damescu is a brilliant scientist, and former employee of Adrian Malprave. Before working for Malprave, Damescu was a leading researcher of DNA sampling and cloning. Possibly fearing retribution after resigning from her post, Damescu fled to the British Embassy in Bucharest, and is said to be carrying a Data Chip with information on an Identicon special project known only as Poseidon. You must contact and rescue her as she could provide vital information. But be on the lookout; Interpol has informed us that professional terrorist Carla the Jackal may be out to capture Damescu on Malprave's behalf.

Reginald Griffin

Reginald Griffin is a British diplomat at the British Embassy in Bucharest, Romania. He's been acting suspiciously, and he has been the subject of a thorough Foreign Ministry investigation. He is believed to be somewhere within the secure area of the British Embassy in Bucharest, intent on protecting a "secure room"–a zone of the Embassy outside his authority. He may be hiding something, but because he is a high-ranking official, you must handle this covertly–many of the people he commands may think you're a threat.

British Embassy Soldiers

The British Embassy in Bucharest, Romania, is a secure facility patrolled by highly experienced members of the British Armed Forces. These soldiers do not know of your covert mission, and may suspect you as a terrorist when you attempt to enter the Embassy. Therefore, it is vital that you not be seen. If you are spotted, you must subdue these soldiers in a *non-lethal* method.

Enemies

Identicon Corporation is a subsidiary of Malprave Industries. That name has been cropping up frequently in reports from the field during MI6's monitoring of international threats to Britain. MI6 has begun a full investigation of Malprave Industries, and will report its findings to you as they become available. At this point, details are sketchy, but familiarize yourself with the following individuals associated with Identicon and Malprave. Also listed here are the troops, vehicles, and aircraft of Malprave's organization.

Adrian Malprave

Only recently has Adrian Malprave come to the attention of MI6. Malprave has developed Malprave Industries into one of the world's largest and broadest multi-national corporations. Malprave Industries is involved in oil, shipping, and biotechnology. Malprave has recently been photographed with known underworld figures such as Carla the Jackal, and an investigation has revealed that some Identicon subsidiaries have no apparent corporate function or income. We suspect that Malprave is currently in a research facility off the coast of Hong Kong.

Nigel Bloch

Bloch is CEO of Identicon Corporation, a subsidiary of Malprave Industries. He has come under suspicion during the MI6 inquiry into that company. A brilliant engineer and shrewd businessman, Bloch has only a brief dossier in MI6 files. He has apparently led a respectable life with a number of professional successes and citations in the field of biotechnology research. However, his association with Malprave leads MI6 to believe that Bloch has returned to criminal activity. From cursory glances at Bloch's recent movements, he appears to be close to Malprave, overseeing many of Identicon's activities. Keep a close eye on this man—as he may be armed and dangerous.

Carla the Jackal

No one knows the real name of Carla the Jackal—an encounter with her is usually the last. Always available for hire, Carla appears to have a growing relationship with Adrian Malprave. Their intentions are unknown, but she was last known to be in Eastern Europe, possibly on the trail of an ex-Identicon employee named Dr. Damescu. Carla's favored weapon is the Windsor FSU-4.

Bebe and Bella

Bebe and Bella manage security for Malprave Industries and for Adrian Malprave personally. Never far from Malprave's side, they have long criminal records and are considered expert in martial arts and firearms. Don't be swayed by their considerable charms, 007. Approach them both with extreme caution. They were last known to be in Malprave's head office in the Swiss mountains.

Malprave Security Forces

Previous combat operatives have been unable to infiltrate and compromise any of Malprave's secret facilities. This may be due to the number of guards she has that are armed with heavy ammunition.

Malprave Security Force Veterans

Covert combat operatives have noted stronger, more powerful veterans training for combat alongside their lesser brethren. Always without headgear, these troops tend to rush headlong at their foes, firing Shotguns or Machine Guns. This attack style has earned them the nickname Berserker Guards. Backpedal and fire, or strafe around these foes.

Malprave Security Elite Forces

Malprave's security becomes more and more impressive as you progress. They become more proficient at attacking, and more attack you simultaneously. The best of Malprave's forces are the elite guard, said to guard a secret Alpine Base high in the Swiss mountains. These individuals are excellent shots, they work in teams to surround you, and they're armed with the latest automatic weapons. Approach these enemies with extreme caution.

Malprave Vehicular Forces

Malprave has a number of troops specially trained in vehicular combat. Watch out for black sedans and limousines–their drivers weave to avoid your fire, and troops fire Machine Guns and Rockets from the sunroofs. In addition, armored vans thwart your progress–highly experienced soldiers appear from the back shutter-doors to attack with Rockets or bullets. Take out the wheels of these vehicles to minimize the damage you receive.

Attack Helicopters

Malprave also employs civilian helicopters, some-times armed with Rockets and utilizing a single side-mounted troop armed with Machine Guns.

These airborne units are extremely maneuverable, continually fire at your location, and don't give up until you demolish them. Repel helicopters with all available ordnance.

Helicopter Gunships

Helicopter gunships are among Malprave's most dead-ly forces. Bristling with Machine Guns and Rocket chambers, heavily armored, and having almost limit-less combat potential, this mighty airborne unit cause more than headaches for even the most seasoned operative. It does however, have an Achilles' heel–its pilot. Aim a Sniper Rifle bullet at the pilot to down the gunship simply and effectively. If there's no Sniper Rifle available, pepper the gunship with Machine Gun fire.

Throughout your missions, you must utilize a variety of weapons efficiently and effectively. With this in mind, Q-Branch has made available a complete list of ordnance, items, vehicles, and other inventory necessary to complete the task at hand.

Please note that some experimental weaponry being tested at MI6 is only available in multiplayer combat, and is detailed in the Multiplayer chapter. Remember that some weapons also have a secondary firing feature.

Hand-to-Hand Combat

Use hand-to-hand combat whenever possible; it is especially effective when you need to be stealthy. A simple one-two punch in a continuous movement around a victim renders him unconscious in a matter of seconds. Usually, if you sneak up behind an unsuspecting enemy, it will only take a single blow to subdue him. Some enemies even drop extra items that do not appear when you dispatch them using ordnance. Remember, hand-to-hand combat is also your quietest weapon available!

Pistols

Pistols have a relatively slow rate of fire (slower than SMGs or Assault Rifles), pack good hitting power per bullet, and generally have very good accuracy. However, they reload slowly, their damage overall can be low, and they only fire a few bullets before you have to reload. The P2K tends to be more accurate than the Viper or the Defender over large distances.

Wolfram P2K

> **Starting Ammunition: 24 bullets**
> **Chamber/Clip Size: 6 bullets**
> **Rate of Fire: 5 rounds per second**
> **Secondary Feature: Silenced**

Designed to be the next generation of sidearm for the German police, this 9mm Pistol sports a compact design and smooth firing mechanism. The reliable Wolfram P2K is a fine complement to any OO agent.

Bond's Wolfram P2K can be fitted with a silencer that screws into the barrel. To toggle use of the silencer, press SELECT.

The regulation weapon for most missions, the P2K inflicts minimal damage compared to other weapons, but it's fast-firing, and features a silencer. Use the silencer whenever possible–it allows for stealthy infiltrations. Note that the silenced mode is not available in all missions.

Windsor Viper

> **Starting Ammunition: 6**
> **Chamber/Clip Size: 6**
> **Rate of Fire: 2 rounds per second**
> **Secondary Fire: None**

There aren't many Pistols with more firepower than the Windsor Viper. This large, stainless-steel Pistol delivers a .44 Magnum bullet with tremendous penetration power. The Viper is limited by its heavy recoil, which reduces its rate of fire.

Although lacking a secondary feature such as a silencer, this slow but tremendously powerful Pistol allows the user to take down enemies in one or two shots. Use the Viper over close to medium range only.

IAC Defender

> **Starting Ammunition: 6**
> **Chamber/Clip Size: 6**
> **Rate of Fire: 2 rounds per second**
> **Secondary Fire: None**

Developed for the Israeli military, the IAC fires a .44 Magnum shell with reasonable accuracy over shorter ranges, thanks to a gas-powered blowback system. This weapon can devastate targets, but the recoil hinders rapid firing.

This weapon, equally as powerful as the ferocious Viper, is perfect for taking out close- to medium-range enemies that are lightly armed and armored.

Machine Guns

Standard issue to Malprave's troops and devastating at close quarters, Machine Guns are suited to those wishing to attack multiple enemies at mid- to close range without running out of time. This weapon takes down numerous enemies prior to a reload. Of course, fast firing also means rapid bullet usage, so be wary about expending too much ammunition in the combat zone. Generally, SMGs have a very high rate of fire (fastest in the game), light hitting power per bullet, and poor accuracy.

Koffler & Stock KS7

Starting Ammunition: 30
Chamber/Clip Size: 30
Rate of Fire: 12.5 rounds per second
Secondary Fire: None
Auto-Aim: Yes
Crosshairs: Yes
Firing Type: Automatic

Another German police product, the Koffler & Stock KS7 is a light-weight Machine Gun that features a sophisticated air-cooling mechanism. It fires a 9X19mm Luger round.

The KS7 is a basic Machine Gun with none of the finery of its more exotic and powerful brothers, but it's powerful enough to cut down troops in seconds and is fast firing against weaker enemies at close to mid range. However, it lacks a large bullet capacity (you'll be reloading twice as much as with the PS100) and a secondary feature.

Ingalls Type 20

Starting Ammunition: 40
Chamber/Clip Size: 40
Rate of Fire: 13.3 rounds per second
Secondary Fire: None
Auto-Aim: Yes
Crosshairs: Yes
Firing Type: Automatic

Originally designed for urban police use, the Ingalls Type 20 never achieved popularity because of its lack of control. Its high rate of fire is hard to master, and for police use, such a weapon is undesirable. Ironically, it has since become very popular with criminal underworld figures who want to deliver a high number of rounds in a hurry, and aren't afraid of missing.

Rattling off more bullets than its brother the KS7, this is the preferred weapon of the two due to the larger clip size and faster rate of fire. Long-range combat however, is a little tricky, because the bullets spread apart at extreme range.

Calypso P-750

Starting Ammunition: 40
Chamber/Clip Size: 80
Rate of Fire: 14.3 rounds per second
Secondary Fire: None
Auto-Aim: Yes
Crosshairs: Yes
Firing Type: Automatic

The feeding magazine gives the Calypso P-750 an unusual and distinct look. The additional grip and other stability features make it a superior weapon to the Ingalls.

If you need to rack your target in fire, this hefty Machine Gun, with its trademark bulky chamber, gives you all the bullets you need. With a huge capacity and the fastest rate of fire of all the weapons, the Calypso is recommended for all forms of combat except silent and long range. Be warned however, the reloading takes time.

Munitions Belgique PS100

Starting Ammunition: 60
Chamber/Clip Size: 60
Rate of Fire: 15.4 rounds per second
Secondary Fire: None
Auto-Aim: Yes
Crosshairs: Yes
Firing Type: Automatic

Built for the Belgian military, the PS100 is an unusual design that shouldn't work—but it does. The magazine lies along the top of the weapon, with the shells perpendicular to the firing direction. When the trigger is depressed, bullets are dropped, spun, and released at a high rate of fire.

In addition, the PS100 fires faster than the Calypso, but lacks the bullet-storage chamber. However, this is offset by the fact that the gun is quick to reload.

Assault Rifles

Featuring a number of innovative secondary functions, from telescopic lenses to mini Grenade Launchers, the Assault Rifles are essential in many situations. From taking out single enemies behind cover with the Windsor FSU-4 to cutting down targets at long range with the UGW, Assault Rifles possess the finest elements of Machine Guns, and each has its own novel addition. Generally, Assault Rifles are more accurate than SMGs and do more damage, but their rate of fire is lower.

Kazakovich KA-57

Starting Ammunition: 30
Chamber/Clip Size: 60
Rate of Fire: 7.7 rounds per second
Secondary Fire: None
Auto-Aim: Yes
Crosshairs: Yes
Firing Type: Automatic

The most recognizable Assault Rifle in the world, the KA-57 was developed in the 1940s for the Soviet infantry, carried by the Warsaw Pact military forces, and exported around the world. Light and reliable, the KA-57 is easy to use as a single-shot Rifle or automatic weapon. It can also stand up under difficult conditions.

Should you wish to fire single shots, fire once, and the weapon acts like a Pistol. If you want rapid fire, press the trigger constantly for rapid bursts, albeit at a slower rate than any other automatic weapon. The KA-57 is a good stalwart weapon, but you should exchange it for a more technologically advanced weapon at the first opportunity.

NOTE

Please note that when two values are shown, the first refers to the weapon's primary capabilities, and the second to any secondary feature as in Auto-Aim and Crosshairs in the following listings.

Windsor FSU-4

Starting Ammunition: 40
Chamber/Clip Size: 40
Rate of Fire: 11.1/2.0
Secondary Fire: Grenade Launcher
Auto-Aim: Yes/No
Crosshairs: Yes/Yes
Firing Type: Automatic/Projectile

A version of the US Army's standard-issue Assault Rifle, the Windsor FSU-4 is a short-barreled monster. Compact and explosive, this carbine is a weapon for all seasons. The Windsor FSU-4 is also fitted with a Grenade Launcher.

With the Grenade Launcher function, you can seek out enemies behind cover, and the Automatic Rifle can down anything from an infantryman to a helicopter gunship. Switching between the two means you never need another weapon—unless your target is at extreme range.

Meyer-Westlicher UGW

Starting Ammunition: 40
Chamber/Clip Size: 40
Rate of Fire: 11.8 rounds per second
Secondary Fire: Scoped
Auto-Aim: Yes/Yes
Crosshairs: Yes/Yes
Firing Type: Automatic/Zoomed Automatic

While other nations preferred steel and aluminum-alloy weapons, the Austrian Army realized the possibilities of designs based on plastics, and they unveiled this innovative weapon in 1979. Its lightweight design is suitable for more conditions than expected, and it has found quite a following around the world.

An excellent alternative to the SSR 4000 Sniper Rifle and any Machine Gun, the UGW features the best of both worlds—a rapid fire and large spread good against close enemies, and a 3X scope for foes at extreme range. Even though this weapon is less accurate at the farthest limits of the scope, the large fan of fire makes this weapon extremely useful for any situation where you have an enemy in a clear line of sight, no matter at what distance.

Koffler & Stock D-17

Starting Ammunition: 50
Chamber/Clip Size: 50
Rate of Fire: 13.3 rounds per second
Secondary Fire: Scoped
Auto-Aim: Yes/Yes
Crosshairs: Yes/Yes
Firing Type: Automatic/Zoomed Automatic

The revolutionary design from Koffler & Stock may change weapons forever. The D-17 fires caseless ammunition, eliminating the need for case-expulsion systems. Such simplicity of design has resulted in a very light and highly accurate rifle.

Although there's much to be said for the D-17–it is devastatingly quick, has a faster rate of fire than some Machine Guns, and has an excellent scope for tagging long-range enemies–it does rattle through ammunition at a shockingly fast pace. Although this weapon has a zoom function of 4X (compared to the UGW's 3X), and is devastating in quick bursts, it may not be suitable for continuous battle.

Other Ordnance

The remaining weapons vary from Shotguns (the weapons of choice at extremely close range) to the heaviest of weapons (firing projectiles that cause splash damage, affecting both the target and the surrounding area). These weapons have extremely different uses in the combat zone.

Frinesi Special 12 Shotgun

Starting Ammunition: 8
Chamber/Clip Size: 8
Rate of Fire: 0.7 rounds per second
Secondary Fire: Automatic
Auto-Aim: Yes/Yes
Crosshairs: Yes/Yes
Firing Type: Regular/Automatic

One could stop a charging herd with the Frinesi Special 12–but not very accurately. Used by police forces around the world, this 12-gauge combat Shotgun has limited range, yet tremendous firepower.

If you want multiple shots on a single foe, use the secondary feature–it turns the Shotgun into an automatic. (This feature is only available in multiplayer.) If your target is at close or extremely close range, you only need one shot. At over 15 feet away, you need two to three shots, and the weapon is almost useless at anything farther than 15 feet. The automatic feature quickens the appalling reload time, but shortens the range even more!

SWZ SSR 4000 Sniper Rifle

Starting Ammunition: 5
Chamber/Clip Size: 5
Rate of Fire: 0.5 rounds per second
Secondary Fire: Scoped
Auto-Aim: No/No
Crosshairs: Yes/Yes
Firing Type: Regular/Zoomed

A bolt-action rifle, the SSR 4000 can deliver single shots accurately and at great distances. A ventilated stock design assists in diffusing heat during repeated firing. The SSR 4000 is equipped with a 6X telescopic sight.

If you want to take out an enemy at long range, there is nothing better than this weapon. Switch immediately to the secondary feature, and zoom in using the right ana-log stick to pick out an enemy from almost a mile away. When targeting, aim for the lower torso for the best results. Don't use this weapon in close combat–a rapidly moving foe combines with this weapon's slow reload to hinder you at close range.

Culpepper M6HB

Starting Ammunition: Varies
Chamber/Clip Size: Varies
Rate of Fire: 7.7 rounds per second
Secondary Fire: None
Auto-Aim: Yes
Crosshairs: Yes
Firing Type: Automatic

The Culpepper is a unique weapon; it appears within the combat zone attached to a "nest," an Armored plate on a turret. Firing at around the same range as the KA-57, but with much greater damage potential, this weapon can tackle a number of charging foes or a large enemy (such as an attack helicopter) with ease. You can't take it with you, so use it judiciously, and save your own ammunition.

ground, run at it with your Launcher pointed down, then fire and immediately leap. You'll take damage, but clear at least 12 feet in the process. Not employed in single-player, this is a useful multiplayer technique. Wear Armor when you try this move!

MRL-22 Rocket Launcher

> Starting Ammunition: 3
> Chamber/Clip Size: 1
> Rate of Fire: 1 round per second
> Secondary Fire: Tracking Rocket Launcher
> Auto-Aim: No/No
> Crosshairs: Yes/Yes
> Firing Type: Projectile/Projectile

This compact, shoulder-launched weapon delivers unguided Rockets that have tremendous effect in close quarters. You usually acquire this single-shot weapon when a large threat is present–a helicopter gunship. The projectile nature of the ammunition makes precise aiming difficult when facing an enemy–and you are better off to fire where you think the enemy is going, rather than firing at the actual target.

In multiplayer, the secondary function of the Rocket Launcher is to launch a single tracking Rocket. This differs from the regular Rockets in that the shot follows your target crosshairs no matter where they are–so if you sidestep left or right, the Rocket follows. This enables proficient agents to fire around corners.

Splash Damage and Rocket-Jumping

Rockets and grenades cause splash damage; that is, they wound everyone in the immediate area around the target. This enables you to plant projectiles between troops or near to exploding barrels to cause added damage, but keep a safe distance.

In addition, use the Rocket Launcher to gain extra height in a jump by employing a technique known as Rocket-jumping. When you want to jump to higher

Frag Grenades

> Starting Ammunition: 1
> Chamber/Clip Size: 1
> Rate of Fire: 1 rounds per second
> Secondary Fire: None
> Auto-Aim: No
> Crosshairs: Yes
> Firing Type: Projectile

A well-placed Grenade can scatter the opposition and keep them down while you escape. In addition, the trajectory of the Grenade, based on how much you tilt your body up or down before throwing, is extremely important. The height of your throw (unless you're looking directly up–then the Grenade simply travels up and down vertically), and the length of time you hold the Grenade (keep the Grenade after arming it for a longer throw) affect where it lands.

Useful for clearing areas of concentrated troops, the unpredictable nature of the Frag Grenade makes it questionable for novice operatives–novices may aim too high and hit a high beam, causing the Grenade to bounce back.

Q-Dart

> Starting Ammunition: 12
> Chamber/Clip Size: 3
> Rate of Fire: 1 round per second
> Secondary Fire: None
> Auto-Aim: Yes
> Crosshairs: Yes
> Firing Type: Bullet

The Q-Dart delivers a non-lethal shot that renders the victim unconscious for up to two hours. When you must infiltrate an area, but must not harm adversaries, the Q-Dart (also known as the Dartgun) is the weapon of choice. One shot, usually to the outer extremities, does the trick. However, its limited supply of darts makes this primarily a marksman's weapon.

Q-Gadgets

In addition to the many weapons you're equipped with or locate yourself, Q-Branch supplies you with the latest in gadgetry. These items are not offensive weapons, but rather tools to help you progress with minimum difficulty.

Many of these gadgets are attached to what looks like an ordinary mobile phone–many of the devices are experimental, and have yet to see extensive field testing.

Q-Claw

When activated, the Q-Claw extends a double-coiled filament. If the filament strikes a suitable surface, it grabs and holds, pulling the holder of the Q-Claw toward that point. It's very useful in securing entrance to above-ground areas. The Q-Claw is standard issue and is carried in every assignment.

The actual surface needed for the Q-Claw to attach to is easy to spot–it is a small, round, gold mesh with a gold metal surrounding. Locate one of these in a mission, and target it with it point. While the Q-Claw pulls you, you can remove weapons and get ready for combat–the Q-Claw automatically recoils after use, and you can aim it at practically any distance.

Q-Laser

Each OO agent also carries the Q-Laser. When activated, the Q-Laser emits a short-range laser with tremendous cutting power. This tool is useful for breaking locks, opening portals, and snapping chains. The Q-Laser is standard issue for all OO agents and is carried in every assignment.

If you spot a large silver padlock, produce the Q-Laser and cut it. This usually frees a hostage or opens a locked door or hatchway. Be aware that you can't relock a hatchway once opened, so take care when lasering areas underneath you. You can also employ the laser at longer distances and melt any lock you can see clearly.

Q-Specs

These spectacles reveal what's hidden behind doors, hatches, and panels. When activated, they reveal hidden compartments and chambers.

Place the glasses on, and the entire view becomes blue. However, secret panels are shown in a lighter color, and rooms behind the panels are also visible.

Q-Camera

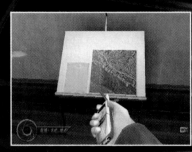

This tiny tool of the spy trade should come in handy. Select the camera and point it so that the subject is in the center of the screen. Press the button to take a snapshot. Fortunately, there is a limitless supply of film for this device, so you may fire off "test" photos prior to snapping pictures of evidence. If you take a photo of particular interest, you will be informed the instant this occurs. Do make sure the object you're photographing is in the middle of the picture!

Q-Remote

A green pulse allows you to either memorize or use the device. A red pulse indicates it can only be used after you find its matching remote, which should be pulsing green. In other words, using the Q-Remote in front of a green pulse will either activate it or allow the Q-Remote to memorize it so you can then activate the matching devices on the level.

Q-Decryptor

Are you having problems with security doors? No Keycards or Computer Access Cards to be found? Then bring up your Q-Decryptor–marvelous for unlocking electronic doors. Not only that, but it can download important data from computers into the bargain! However, don't confuse this item with the Q-Remote–the Q-Decryptor is useful for unlocking doors and gathering information only–it cannot "learn" to unlock or start other devices.

Q-Card

point and activate the Q-Card at any electronic lock. In a few seconds, the Q-Card opens the locking mechanism. If you encounter an electronic lock (*not* a padlock) without a Q-Card, you will not have access. Locate a Q-Card, then open the door.

Q-Jet

The Q-Jet can lift an agent up to the air to reach elevated platforms or locations. Activate the device and off you go. To fly the Q-Jet, use normal movement controls. This may look like a jetpack, but

each batch of compressed air you fill the Q-Jet with (from the numerous compressed-gas filling stations) has only enough power for a single leap. If you don't jump and activate the unit, the jump is wasted. You have some control as you descend, but not much.

Driving Gadgets

You have access to a variety of gadgets as pick-ups. These gadgets serve a variety of purposes; some are highly expensive and last only a single use.

Q-Pulse

The Q-Pulse emits an electromagnetic shock wave that disables electronic devices within its radius. Since most vehicles operate with electronically controlled fuel injection systems, the Q-Pulse stops them in their tracks. The device charges for a second, then emits the shockwave. The enemy vehicle

must be within a few meters for the device to work.

Q-Vision

Q-Vision goggles reveal all sources of heat. They are a good means of detecting a running engine in the dark, or an enemy lurking on a rooftop. Enemy infantry and vehicles appear bright green. As soon as you see them, target and fire at them. This device has an

Q-Smoke

Use Q-Smoke to put up a smoke screen. Remember to throw it behind you. Q-Smoke emits a cloud of white smoke designed to confuse the enemy.

Q-Slick

This oily concoction sends vehicles sliding a long way. The Q-Slick is best employed on corners, where there is maximum chance of an enemy car driving over the slick.

Q-Booster

For an extra burst of speed, use the Q-Booster to accelerate for a period of no more than three seconds. The turbo boost allows you to clear ramps with ease and catch up with enemies. Use the Q-Booster with care—the increase in speed is instantaneous, and can lead to loss of control!

Items

Finally, there are a number of items that are sometimes vital, and always useful. When you obtain them, they are automatically applied to your inventory, weapon, or Armor. If you cannot carry them (due to your inventory being stocked full of a particular item), the object remains in view.

Armor

These suits of padded Kevlar body Armor increase your damage resistance as shown on the Armor Meter. Each hit you take removes a unit from your Armor Meter. Only pick up

Armor after you neutralize all immediate threats—you can return to pick up Armor if you need it later. Beware: Armor is sparse.

Dropped Weapons and Ammo Clips

Every human enemy drops a weapon—usually a gun. Picking up dropped weapons is the only way to build up your arsenal, so when you down an enemy, check the area for his weapon.

You may wish to stay in populated areas to take out more bad guys and collect more ammunition for your weapons. If you find a weapon you already have, you gain ammunition instead of a duplicate weapon.

Other Items

There are many other items that you must use in specific situations in specific levels. The walkthrough details these types of objects, such as Computer Access Cards, Keycards, and Briefcases.

Vehicles

In the missions ahead, the latest in vehicular design couples with Q-Branch advancements to make the perfect car for you. Take a moment to brush up on the vehicles under your command.

Aston Martin DB5

MI6 has outfitted its fleet of Aston Martin DB5s with bulletproof plating, front-mounted weapons, and rear-deployed defense mechanisms. Our Engine Works has improved and tuned the classic Alu S6 DOHC engines so that there is no performance

drop-off due to the increased weight. However, the age of this vehicle affects its performance; it doesn't corner quite as quickly as the latest German automobiles.

BMW Z8

This vehicle's five-liter V8 engine powers this lightweight car to 60mph in less than 5 seconds. Top speed approaches 150mph. It also comes standard with front-mounted Machine Guns and Rockets, and can be fitted with a variety of additional power-ups, just like the

Aston Martin. The Z8's cornering ability is a little tighter, and the control a little less sluggish than that of the Aston Martin.

Other Vehicles

Three other vehicles are available to you: a BMW 750il, an MGF-34 Battle Tank (complete with Chain Gun and Cannon), and a hover tram. Remember—these vehicles aren't invincible, and it's your job to take down the enemy before they damage these expensive pieces of machinery beyond repair.

Driving/Rail Shooting Weapons

Naturally, Q-Branch has endeavored to make your driving experience as pleasant as possible. Should you encounter an enemy threat, utilize the following weapons and equipment.

CH-6 Mini Rocket Launcher

This Rocket Launcher projects unguided Missiles wherever you point it. It only comes equipped with six Rockets, so save this for multiple targets appearing at once.

It also has a controllable missile variant, the RCH-1, useful for destroying narrow structures that a Rocket must be negotiated through.

KA-57S Assault Rifle

The S stands for "scope." With the scope attachment, this Assault Rifle becomes a fine weapon for aiming at specific areas (such as the tires on a enemy sedan). It is the favored weapon for vehicular combat settings until you acquire Rockets.

12-Gauge Shotgun

This 12-Gauge Shotgun variant is an alternative to the KA-57S, and inflicts more damage per shot. However, it is slow to use and reload. It also has "zooming" capabilities, but is less effective at longer distances. Only employ it in situations where you can aim carefully, or when you run out of KA-57 ammunition.

Chain Gun

While riding the battle tank, spend the majority of combat using the Chain Gun, a rapid-fire, belt-fed device with more than enough ammunition for the task at hand. The gun can be used with a scope, providing offensive and covering fire.

Tank Cannon

The Tank Cannon clears your tank's path when two or three vehicles attack at the same time. Only target a couple of large threats before reverting back to the Chain Gun, because the Tank Cannon's limited ammunition means you should save it for the final targets in a mission.

Car-Mounted Machine Guns

Attached to your car, these Machine Guns are useful for lining up shots with your unguided Rockets. Inflicting reasonable but unimpressive damage, these are only really useful to complement an attack with a more powerful weapon.

Car-Mounted Rockets

Line up your shot with Machine Gun fire; these Rockets aren't cheap! For best results, fire at where your enemy will likely be when the Rocket hits, not where he is at the moment.

Car-Mounted Guided Missiles

You use the Car-Mounted Guided Missiles during missions three and seven. The Missiles track any target; the Missile's target is indicated in blue. Remember, although these Missiles are guided, bridges, narrow buildings, and other scenery (such as lampposts) impede the Missile's trajectory. For the best results, fire with a clear line of sight.

Trouble in Paradise

MI6 Briefing

007, the CIA has come to us for assistance. It appears that one of their agents–a Ms. Zoe Nightshade–recently sent out a distress signal. The girl is clearly in trouble, and since you're already on location in Hong Kong, we saw this as an opportunity to help out our American cousins in the CIA.

Ms. Nightshade was leading an undercover investigation of a biogenetic research firm known as Identicon. This company is headed by Nigel Bloch, a suspected global criminal kingpin. The CIA believes that Identicon is a front for a massive smuggling ring dealing in terrorist bio-weapons.

In Nightshade's last report, she mentioned that Identicon had taken considerable security measures to protect a metal case containing a number of vials. She intended to steal the case to get its contents analyzed, but her mission was compromised at the last minute. You need to find that case, and rescue Ms. Nightshade.

R has provided you with new equipment. First is the Q-Claw, a high-tension grapple line that allows you to latch onto special surfaces and pull yourself up to ledges and platforms. You also carry the Q-Laser, which emits a powerful beam of coherent light, capable of slicing through certain metals.

OBJECTIVES

1. Infiltrate Research Facility
2. Find courier case containing vials
3. Rescue CIA Agent Zoe Nightshade

Classified Information–Mission Overview

Bond clambers onto a helipad outside the facility, and watches as a business-suited executive appears from his company helicopter (model G-8VO) carrying a reinforced medical case with the Identicon logo on it.

This facility is split into three sections–the Entrance Deck, the Research Laboratory, and the Docks. Each is peppered with an increasing number of Identicon henchmen, but the use of scenery (both to hide behind and as a devastating weapon) is the key to victory. Use force when necessary, but keep your trigger finger at bay once Ms. Nightshade is located–one stray shot could spell disaster.

Entrance Deck

You start high above the sea on a helipad. Check out the enormous research facility and the view of Hong Kong through the orange haze. Then check the facility corridor to the left of the security door.

There's a small side room that is impervious to your P2K–remember where this chamber is–it houses exceptional ordnance that you come back for later. Inspect the door and the antenna above.

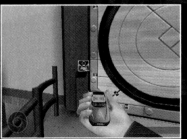

As you climb the steps to the door, R chimes in from HQ to recommend a course of action–Q-Clawing up onto the roof or using your Q-Decryptor on the complex door lock.

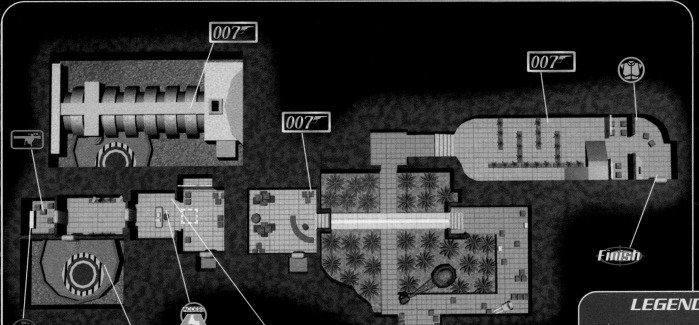

- **Start** - *Start*
- - *Alarm Button*
- - *Frag Grenade*
- - *Rocket Launcher*
- **007** - *007 Bonus*
- - *Armor*
- **ACCESS** - *Armory Keycard*
- - *Zoe Nightshade*
- **Finish** - *Finish*

As you step into the entrance corridor, a remote camera spots you. Identicon knows of your presence! You cannot destroy the camera or open the door to the left. Instead, go down the corridor to the second secure door.

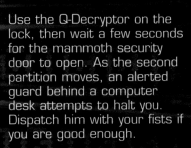

Use the Q-Decryptor on the lock, then wait a few seconds for the mammoth security door to open. As the second partition moves, an alerted guard behind a computer desk attempts to halt you. Dispatch him with your fists if you are good enough.

If you're quick, you can subdue the guard before he raises the alarm. Otherwise, you'll be fighting with a siren blaring in the background. After you defeat the guard, turn off the alarm.

BEING BOND

The best way to enter this facility is to keep your arrival secret. Stealth is the key. From your starting position, look up, and step back until you spot the silver mesh on the antenna above the entrance door. Aim and fire your Q-Claw at it.

BEING BOND

CONTINUED

Aim the Q-Claw so it attaches to the bottom portion of the mesh. Once at the top, check out the view of Hong Kong's business district, then turn and run along the narrow roof balcony.

At the end of the roof, drop down into a small alcove above the guard. As you fall, turn 180 degrees and watch the guard type for a moment. Duck down, and ready your fists. Although a shot with the P2K is tempting, do not try it; alerting him to your presence jeopardizes this part of the mission.

Once on the ground, sneak up behind the guard and execute one swift punch. The guard crumples to the ground, dropping a fully loaded P2K. On the terminal next to him is a Keycard. Pick it up. You only receive the Keycard if you dispatch the guard without him seeing you.

Firing at the guard, moving into his field of vision, or entering via the helipad door alerts the guard, and you cannot retrieve the Keycard. With the Q-Decryptor primed, move to the door and unlock it. Then jog down the entrance corridor. Ignore the secure door to the helipad.

The camera doesn't spot you, so run quickly to the locked door to the Armory (you spotted the room from the helipad earlier) with the red-lit lock, and unlock it. A storage room is behind the door. Inside, you find an MRL-22 Rocket Launcher (armed with three Rockets), and four Frag Grenades.

Whether you infiltrated the Armory or not, there is only one way forward—into a spectacular viewing area. Ahead is a massive greenhouse, under which a tropical rainforest grows. Ignore the boxes and head for the elevator to the right. Activate it.

Research Laboratory I

Equip the P2K, and wait until the elevator stops. A second guard is on duty at his computer terminal. If you haven't been discovered yet, a second remote camera spots you. Now attack the enemy.

Two swift shots from your P2K are enough to take down the guard. Alternatively, you will score better if you can run around and punch him. Another option is to wait for him to hide behind some crates near the barrel. One shot into the barrel and it's goodnight for this ex-Identicon employee.

Rounding the corner of the computer terminal, find a padlocked door. Select your Q-Laser, and aim the green bolt of light at the lock. After a couple of seconds, the lock breaks. Head through the door.

In the hallway encased in bulletproof glass, you can see another corridor below you. Head to the other side, moving cautiously until you spot the guard who's keeping watch. Then aim carefully....

Now move down the ramp and turn the corner. You're faced with a ramped corridor heading down, with boxes and soil bags scattered about. At the end of the ramp, two soldiers (three if you missed the first one) crouch behind cover. Nearby, a forklift holds a large red canister.

As soon as the action starts, point your Pistol at the red canister, and fire (preferably without using your crosshairs, or you may be hit). If you strike the canister, it explodes, demolishing the forklift and sending the guards reeling. Good job, 007!

BEING BOND

If you're sure of yourself, you can advance down the ramp with your Pistol, aiming at each guard. Pick up their dropped KS7s and switch to this weapon. Stick with the KS7 for now—it comes in handy in a moment.

Other methods of foe disposal include lobbing grenades down the ramp, or leveling the field with a well-aimed rocket. But try not to overdo things.

Around the corner, you encounter a ramp down, a group of crates, and another box suspended from a crane cable. Behind the far set of boxes on the right-hand side is another enemy. Run down the ramp and deal with him.

BEING BOND

You can also incapacitate your adversary by aiming up and shooting the cable, dislodging the crate. Watch as it hits the guard's head, knocking him out. Very clever, 007!

As you pass the final set of boxes on your right, another four of Identicon's entry-level henchmen run down the corridor. The easiest tactic is to wait just around the corner and engage them as they run into view.

BEING BOND

Alternative methods of dealing with the quartet of guards? Leap out around the corner of the long corridor immediately, and engage the enemies as they run forward. Duck behind the wall to avoid their fire.

Or, step back into the garage alcove, grab the Armor, duck, confront them individually.

Finally, you can always back up to the forklift, firing as you go, and advancing at the squad as they attempt to defend. If you've failed to explode the canister, you can even retreat to the initial hallway, wait for the guards to head for cover, and blow up the forklift.

When the guards are gone, run down the corridor. You appear in the central laboratory area, with dozens of orchids growing in a climate-controlled environment.

Research Laboratory II

As you step forward, the lights go out, plunging the laboratory into darkness, save for the halogen lamps. A total of seven guards have laid an ambush for you.

Time to run—head through the entrance and sidestep left, using the foliage as cover.

You hear shouts from the guards ahead. Ignore these yells, and methodically take them on. Sidestep right, facing the guards, and step around the first set of planters, then sidestep to the second wall buttress. Aim and fire at guards as you spot them.

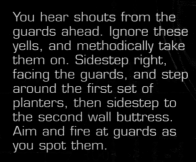

Listen for guards. If a grenade lands nearby, run away from it, using the plants as cover and moving past the two planters to your right, to the third wall buttress. At some point, one or two guards may come to investigate. Deal with them quickly.

Head around the single planter while the bullets fly, and head behind the final buttress. By now, you should be able to see, aim at, and dispatch the guard crouching in the opposite corner behind the planters, plus the remaining guards in the main area.

You're left with the two guards hiding behind the crates. Peek around the buttress and attempt to aim at them, or rush their positions. Pick up the Shotgun, and arm yourself with it.

Enter the exit bay, illuminated in red. The final guard hides behind a crate, next to a piece of Body Armor. One accurate blast with the Shotgun should do the trick. Quickly turn and head for the door, picking up the case containing the vials. Now to find Ms. Nightshade....

BEING BOND

Need a better way to pass through this laboratory? As you move through the entrance, head right, crouch (L2), and creep past the five planters along the right wall. Guards are easy to aim at and you won't find yourself confused or hemmed in, and the cover is excellent!

The Docks

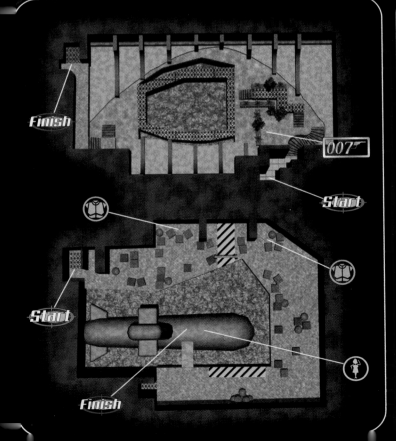

Out of the door, you head up the winding steps into a mammoth hangar. Stepping forward, Bond spots a guard sniper training his laser sights on the incapacitated Ms. Nightshade while three henchmen patrol below. Time to deal with that tricky marksman.

Head up the shallow metal steps onto the gangplank, and walk toward the railing above the hangar. It seems Bloch has captured Nightshade and is intent on her demise. The submarine she's tied to will submerge in five minutes!

Run onto the walkway with the sniper, and head straight for him, taking him down with bullets or fists (preferable) as he drops his SSR 4000 Sniper Rifle to reload a Pistol for close-quarters fighting. As the sniper falls, a siren sounds–Bloch's men have spotted you!

LEGEND

Start - Start

007 - 007 Bonus

- Armor

- Zoe Nightshade

Finish - Finish

BEING BOND

Even before Bond spots Nightshade, he can load up with the Rocket Launcher, aim, and fire at the sniper, or tag the sniper with his KS7 after the cutscene. The guard staggers backwards, falling off the railing and landing on a platform below.

Once you've retrieved the Sniper Rifle, run toward the opposite side of the walkway, down the steps, and across the balcony. Hug the left wall and avoid being shot. Dive into the elevator, and activate it.

At the end of the balcony, run into the elevator and quickly activate it. As the elevator descends, sidestep quickly out. Run to the garage, ready to battle the remaining guards.

BEING BOND

Battling through the top tier of the hangar is easy, but the main battle lies below, with 10 of Identicon's finest ready to attack you.

If you've been less than successful with your Sniper Rifle, you'll have to dodge a massive amount of crossfire. Move methodically. Start by stepping out of the garage door cover and turning left to tag the first guard.

Arm the Sniper Rifle, aiming at mid-range rather than close range. Instead of moving onto the walkway (where you'll be shot) to fire, use the metal steps you just descended as cover, aiming and taking down enemies at the far side. Crouch in front of the steps to locate enemies you can only partially see.

Run to the concrete pillar on the left wall and destroy the barrel near the second guard, or engage the soldier if he's too far from the explosion. Then sidestep right, away from the concrete pillar, and take down the soldier behind the boxes by aiming at the next barrel you see.

TIP

Destroy any barrels you see; the enemy also aims for them, and relaxing near a detonating cask of explosives isn't advisable.

You have five Sniper Rifle shots—hit with each one. Then switch to the Rocket Launcher or Frag Grenades and run along the balcony, lobbing or firing at any remaining henchmen. Aim at the barrels for extra explosions. Remember to hold Grenades for a couple of seconds before throwing to add range.

Take out the barrel near the stack of large boxes, or the enemy will as you pass it. Hug the left wall, running around some boxes to snag a suit of Body Armor. Then take cover behind the second large concrete pillar, peeking out from behind it.

The next guard lobs a Frag Grenade at you. Duck back behind the pillar or run straight for him, but be accurate with your aim. Retreat behind the last concrete pillar, take out the barrel next to the second suit of Body Armor at range, and pick the armor up if you need it.

Behind here is another guard hiding behind a box and a barrel. If he's still there, you will be forced to confront him. There will then be one guard forward of your position to deal with.

Heading for the corner, you spot another guard running for the two crates. He'll reach the crates before you; you'll be forced to deal with him swiftly.

NOTE

Two great white sharks swim about the submarine, ready to tear apart any secret agent who fails to save Ms. Nightshade. After five minutes, the submarine starts to submerge, so don't waste precious time!

The final two henchmen head out of the elevator, which locked behind them. Wait until they venture into the area with the three barrels, then aim at the exploding containers, hopefully bagging both henchmen with a minimum of fuss.

After disposing of the guards, quickly run down the gangplank and around Zoe Nightshade. She's manacled to the submarine mast. Produce your Q-Laser and aim it at the lock (don't worry–Zoe isn't harmed by it). After a second, she's free.

TIP

Don't shoot Zoe Nightshade as you're freeing her–keep your finger off the trigger button!

With Zoe Nightshade free from shackles, she and Bond escape. Good work, 007. Now check your ranking.

Precious Cargo
Driving Level

MI6 Briefing

Good work on your successful infiltration of the research facility. As you know, your liberation of Agent Nightshade did not go undetected. Bloch's men have been ordered to apprehend you at all costs.

Your destination is Identicon's factory near the dockyards. Agent Nightshade has indicated that the second shipment with the last set of vials can be found there. Penetrate their defenses and recover that case.

Once you have recovered the vials, deliver them to R for analysis. He will be waiting for you within the dockyards and will escort Agent Nightshade to safety.

OBJECTIVES
1. Infiltrate Identicon facility
2. Locate missing vials

Classified Information–Mission Overview

Welcome to Hong Kong, 007. Watch out for the rickshaws and narrow streets, and for goodness sake, avoid civilian casualties. If you go on a shooting rampage and target non-Identicon vehicles, you'll fail the mission.

You'll be targeting Identicon troops as Ms. Nightshade does the driving. You must destroy the enemy threats they it appear. Target the tires rather than shooting enemies directly.

Hong Kong Roadway–Dusk

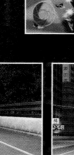

As the mission begins, aim up and locate the helicopter flying in from behind the rocky outcrop. As it nears you, a side gunner opens fire. If you refrain from shooting, the helicopter takes a couple of well-placed shots, moves past you, and leaves.

Otherwise, concentrate all of your KA-57 gunfire at the side gunner and the side of the helicopter. After a couple of seconds of constant fire, the gunner tumbles out of the helicopter and the helicopter explodes. Quickly reload.

Zoe runs over a CH-6 Rocket Pack in the middle of the road. Don't use it yet. Instead, focus on the second helicopter ahead that's firing rockets at you. As Zoe tries to evade the shots by steering the car from side to side, take the helicopter down with KA-57 fire–keep the helicopter in the center of the screen, or let the auto-aim be your guide.

TIP

Take on the helicopter with KA-57 fire until it explodes. Switching to the rockets or shotgun isn't wise; both are difficult to target with.

With continuous well-placed gunfire, the helicopter can be downed before you pass under it. Even if it's not, continue

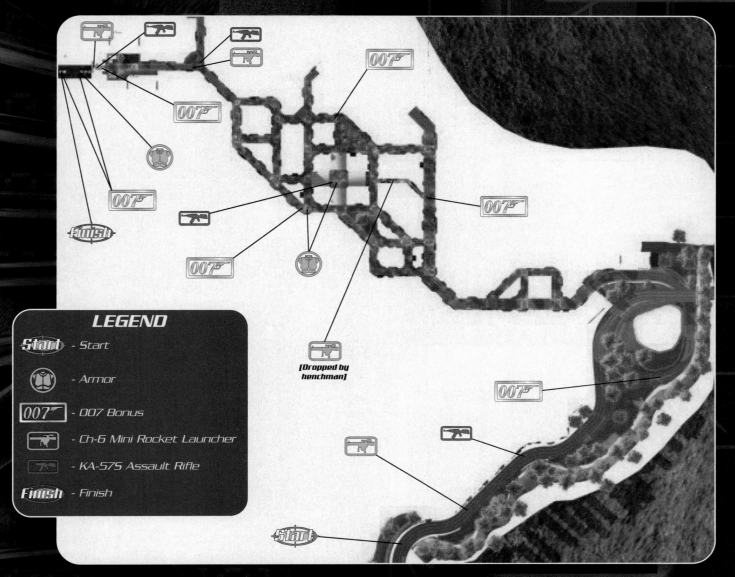

LEGEND

Start - Start

- Armor

007 - 007 Bonus

- Ch-6 Mini Rocket Launcher

- KA-57S Assault Rifle

Finish - Finish

[Dropped by henchman]

to fire at it (aim at the cockpit or the sides) until it explodes. If you ignore it, it continues to take potshots with Machineguns, and a side gunner peppers you with gunfire until your BMW is rendered inoperable.

As you pass the bend where the second helicopter appeared, you see a sedan speeding toward the rear of your car. Aim at the tires until both the enemy on the roof and the vehicle itself are incapacitated.

NOTE

Use the Shotgun or the KA-57 to take out one of the sedan's front tires while the vehicle is still at a distance. This halts the vehicle, and adds to your score. When the sedan closes in, aim for the engine and the tires.

Aiming only for the enemy sticking out of the sunroof diminishes your chances of receiving an excellent score, so keep this in mind when facing enemy vehicles.

As soon as you've finished off the sedan, turn and face the front. Zoe tells you there's an armored van incoming. Blow the tires out with the KA-57 or the Shotgun.

The back shutter of the van opens, revealing a Machine Gun wielding foe. Tag him, then try to take out a second tire.

Be quick about taking out the sedan—a couple of streets later, a limo pulls out from behind you, and begins offensive maneuvers in your direction. Rake the front of the car with KA-57 gunfire, or pop the tires with two Shotgun blasts.

BEING BOND

For this van, aim at two tires and plug away until both are blown out. Sometimes the van crashes into a wall, but usually it continues to run, slowing down and allowing Zoe to pass it. Now the van is no longer a threat—the gunfire only erupts from the back door. Reload just after tagging the first enemy; you don't want to be fiddling for ammunition when a Rocket Launcher is aimed at you.

Just after dealing with the sedan, Zoe turns onto a main street and informs you of a roadblock ahead. Two limos are blocking your path. Bond tells her to turn left. Don't bother hitting the limos (unless you're gunning for a 007 logo); you automatically screech to the left down a narrow market street, knocking carts and sending pedestrians scurrying. Hit the henchman at the end of the alleyway; he'll drop some more CH-6 ammo for you.

As you move out of the narrow alleyway, you spot a sedan in the distance. This is part of an Identicon welcoming committee. Change to your CH-6, and fire two rockets at the sedan as you close.

After dispatching the van, continue to look behind you. As Zoe enters a marketplace, a sedan pulls out of a side street to your left and attacks you. React by taking out one or both front tires, and strafe the radiator grill, taking it out of commission.

As Zoe stops, note the sedan on the left, and the group of henchmen standing around crates to the right. Hit the barrels to the left of the sedan, and watch it explode. Then turn and aim at the barrels by the bad guys to your right. An explosion will ensue, destroying all four men. Zoe revs up the car and continues.

Once you've destroyed the boxes scattered about and there are no more immediate threats, Zoe accelerates wildly and heads to the right. Pick up 200 rounds of KA-57 ammunition and Armor in this area.

When the cut scene ends, aim at the gas pump to the left of the stationary van. Plug it until the gas station explodes in a gigantic ball of fire, incapacitating the van. Then turn to the helicopter and rake it until it explodes. Finally, aim at the two sedans, raking the front tire of the right-hand one, and strafing left until it explodes, taking the second sedan with it. Congratulations—you've just taken out Identicon's finest in 10 seconds flat!

BEING BOND

Rockets are amusingly devastating in this fire fight, but you may want to conserve your CH-6 rockets for the final section of this level. If not, fire one rocket at the helicopter, one at the fuel pump, and two more at the sedans.

Out of the garage, you just have enough time to spot a helicopter heading left before a limo closes in from behind. Expect a bumpy ride through the park. Again, aim for the front two tires for more points, and ignore the enemy peeking out of the sunroof.

Back on the Hong Kong side streets, another sedan barrels into view behind you. Shoot the tires with the Shotgun or rake the front end and tires with the KA-57. This soon sees off this final sedan.

Reload your KA-57, and turn to face the front. After weaving through a couple more streets, Zoe informs you of a large Identicon road-block ahead. This would spell trouble…if there weren't a gas station directly behind the enemy lines!

While Zoe races away from the scene of devastation, tag the van if it's still moving (shotgun blasts at the wheels slow it to a crawl). Aim ahead to the three henchmen at the entrance of the factory; the KA-57s should make short work of them. Pick up another CH-6 Rocket Pack to gain six more rounds. Zoe crashes through the main entrance and into the factory.

The initial enemy in this area is ahead of you on a gangplank. Shoot him with a single Shotgun or Rocket blast, then aim at the three or four other guards on the distant balcony. Use the auto-aim as your guide, and tag each guard as he appears. Rockets work well here.

Once you've downed the henchmen and possibly destroyed a large piece of factory machinery, Zoe starts the car, and you head down some steps. At the bottom are three guards—two on the right, one on the left. One rocket is enough to take down all three—your other weapons aren't quick enough to get them all.

Steady as she goes, 007—after an explosion to your left, shoot at both of the henchman that fire rockets at you from a high platform. Two Rockets or a couple of shotgun blasts work well, as does auto-aim—don't manually use the crosshair for the rest of this sortie. Turn to your right to see the henchman parked in front of the rotating fan; a quick shotgun blast will take care of him.

Once under the gantry, Bond and Zoe appear in a generator room. Take down the guard that appears from behind the left set of crates, then shoot the barrel to eliminate the two in the middle, and finally the three on the right. These are simple one-shot takedowns with the

Shotgun, or a rapid-fire KA-57 spattering. Take these henchmen out before completing your next mission objective.

With all the henchmen disposed of, fire at the large red control switch to the right of the containers. This moves a large container above the generator. Now fire at the crane holding the container—shoot the wires just above the crate. This drops the container onto the generator, effectively crippling the base.

This also opens the previously inaccessible door in front of the car. It slides open, revealing the case with the missing vials. Bond quickly takes these and escapes—the entire facility is exploding! Zoe launches what's left of the BMW through a plate-glass window, and completes the mission in a typically understated manner.

Dangerous Pursuit
Driving Level

MI6 Briefing

007–It's too late for Agent Nightshade, but she needn't have died in vain. It's imperative that you reclaim those vials as quickly as possible.

We've intercepted their radio transmission–they intend to transfer the vials to an armored van for more secure transportation. You must get to the rendezvous before they escape!

Should you be unable to prevent the transfer from occurring, you must stop the armored van at all costs. Use caution, however–we need those vials intact.

R has airdropped some Q-Lab equipment into your area; it will appear as blips on your radar. The Q-Pulse is particularly effective at disabling vehicles without damaging their contents. You'll need to get within a few meters of your target and allow adequate charge-up time to ensure success.

OBJECTIVES
1. Locate stolen vials
2. Disable armored van

Classified Information–Mission Overview

Your skills will be tested in this mission, because you're in control of both the driving and the shooting. You must multi-task effectively, dealing with enemies while searching for and then disabling an armored van.

To assist you in this sortie, concentrate on the map display in the top right corner of your screen–this guides you to the van's location. Along the way, pick up as many Q gadgets as you can, but don't veer off hunting objects–a speedy completion is preferable to a gadget-filled car. Learn to use the Q-Booster and Q-Pulse effectively. Finally, 007, you are free to drive through the city streets in any direction–the notes here are simply the quickest way to achieve success.

Hong Kong Roadway–Dusk

Gun the engine on your BMW Z8–the acceleration is most impressive. M informs you that the stolen briefcase is emitting a tracking signal from the northeast.

LEGEND
Start - Start
- Armor
007 - 007 Bonus
- Ch-6 Mini Rockets
- Missiles
- Q-Booster
- Q-Smoke
- Q-Pulse
Finish - Finish

pr\imagames.com

33

Accelerate down the Docks, turning slightly right, and run over the small white tank containing Q-Smoke. This comes in handy later.

TIP

When you're chased by enemy vehicles, simply slam on the e-brake, and either spin 180 degrees to attack the vehicles or wait until the enemies pass you, then reverse straight backwards and engage them.

Ready your Rockets, and launch them (along with Machine Gun fire) as you pass under the second crane and spot two sedans blocking your way in the distance. To the left of them on a container is a henchman armed with a rocket launcher. Train your fire at the barrels to the left left of the sedan; the splash damage downs all the henchman and leaves some Rockets. You don't need to pick them up—speed away from the roadblock.

If you miss with the Rockets and the sedans are still functioning, they launch rockets at your rear once you pass them. When you hear the "whoosh!" of a rocket closing in, swerve side to side until you turn a slight right and pass the factory on your left side.

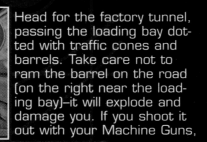

Head for the factory tunnel, passing the loading bay dotted with traffic cones and barrels. Take care not to ram the barrel on the road (on the right near the loading bay)—it will explode and damage you. If you shoot it out with your Machine Guns,

it will dispose of the henchmen there, and reward you with Bond Move points. Once out of the bay, turn right.

BEING BOND

If you're being followed by one of the waterfront sedans you just rammed, slow down a touch, then launch Q-Smoke out of the rear of your vehicle. This incapacitates the enemy driver, allowing you to escape. You could turn and fire at the enemy instead, but this wastes valuable time.

R lets you know exactly what those yellow blips on the HUD map represent. Follow the road as it curves left, and at the next junction, pick up the Q-Pulse object, turn right, and then almost immediately turn left. This is the quickest way to intercept the vials and collect the most items.

After the hard left, continue down this narrow road for one block, then turn right. You career over a paved pedestrian area. Stay left of the giant tree, and run over the Q-Booster.

At the next junction, turn right. Straight ahead is a case containing six Missiles. Run over it immediately, and then slow to turn sharply left onto the main thoroughfare. You'll stay on this road for a while.

BEING BOND

The rule of thumb for riding around Hong Kong and crashing into objects is that lampposts, signs, and traffic lights are all fair game—they can be hit without incurring damage. However, ram a tree and you'll come to an embarrassing halt. Avoid the greenery and civilian traffic—damaging cars will lead to mission failure.

A couple of blocks down the main road, you spot a case of Rockets nestled just behind a traffic light. Grab the Rockets, then continue on your merry way, turning right as the road curves in that direction.

As you approach the turn in the road, you'll need to head right, but first find the Armor in the gas station on the left-hand side of this junction. Pick up the Armor, then spin the car around to face the right and accelerate down the right-hand road.

NOTE

Zipping through the gas station is a task requiring refined driving; don't ram the pumps or launch Rockets at them—the ensuing blast will cause you considerable damage!

The tracking beacon embedded in the briefcase should now be visible as a green flashing light on your map—follow the road as it bends left, and you'll spot the armored van carrying the vials make a break for it, flanked by two sedans.

The van takes off down a side street to your left. Follow it—if you lose sight of it or you're more than a block away from it, the missions is over. Ready your Missiles, and take that sharp left after the van!

Keep one eye on the van, and launch Missiles at the two sedans flanking it—it takes two Missiles to destroy each car. Try not to be in the blast area when the Missile connects—you can be hit by collateral damage, and this affects your point total.

TIP

If a sedan is chasing you, switch to Missiles and your rear view, and then launch—the Missile targets the car behind you (if you can see the car). Alternatively, use the Q-Smoke to disable pursuing forces.

BEING BOND

Now that the van is in your sights, the remainder of the mission is simple—accelerate up to the van, preferably by using the Q-Booster, and then unleash the Q-Pulse (you must be within two car lengths of the van for this weapon to be effective). After a second of charging, the pulse is activated and captures the van in an electromagnetic bubble. The mission is complete! Congratulations!

The remainder of the mission consists of chasing the van, demolishing sedans and limos, and gearing up to Q-Pulse the van off the road. Do not fire at the van—if the van is damaged, the briefcase may be destroyed, and we need those vials intact!

Q-Smoke is an underrated weapon–use it at least once before the chase is over, usually when sedans are chasing you. If you cover both the sedans and the van in smoke, expect an excellent score.

Finding it difficult to use the Q-Booster and Q-Pulse combination? Then try to catch the van by cutting it off at corners. The van usually takes wide turns and isn't quite as fast as your Z8. Stay to the inside (sometimes dodging traffic), and you'll catch it at the next bend.

Sometimes the van takes a sharp right, heading into a subway system. Follow the van down, driving onto the tracks and staying left. Swerve to the middle to snag the Armor. Then hug the right wall on the way onto the platform to avoid the trains.

Just after you emerge from the subway, the van follows the road as it bends left, and then attempts to lose you by turning sharply left. You can either slam on the brakes and follow it, or attempt to enter a nearby hotel–it's the building with the Q-Booster marquee in front of the doors on the first corner after the subway exit.

Smash through the hotel doors, head up the escalator, and drive straight through the upstairs window. You

emerge on a narrow rooftop across from the hotel. Keep the pedal to the metal and follow the roof path, picking up the Armor, and then plough straight through the wooden billboard at the end. After a long and impressive aerial jump, you land directly behind the van. Now is the time to execute the Q-Pulse.

BEING BOND

Is ramming a billboard not enough of a thrill? Then execute a Q-Booster while you're on the roof, and keep your car steady. If you hit the billboard, you can actually land ahead of the van, allowing you to Q-Smoke it for extra points, and then Q-Pulse it.

If you're finding it difficult to line up your rockets with an enemy in front of you, use the Machine Guns in your Z8 to line up your fire, and then unleash those rockets.

MI6 Briefing

The briefcase you retrieved contained nine vials of human blood samples, as well as photographs of the British Embassy in Romania. Eight of the vials were labeled with the initials of the world's leading industrial nations. The last vial was marked GRIFFIN.

A computer database search has turned up a man named Reginald Griffin serving as a British diplomat in Romania. Griffin's recent behavior has been the subject of an internal Foreign Ministry report. In particular, he seems obsessed with protecting a "secure room" in the Embassy—an area outside his jurisdiction.

Infiltrate Griffin's secure room, find out what he's hiding, and access his computer records. Griffin is a personal friend of the Prime Minister, so this must remain a strictly covert investigation. Remember, too, that the guards are not suspected and may not be harmed.

R has provided you with a special Dartgun, which will tranquilize but not harm the guards. In addition to your standard gadgets, R has issued you a pair of Q-Specs, which can be used to see hidden doors and hatches. These may come in handy.

OBJECTIVES

1. Infiltrate private quarters on top floor
2. Gain access to secure room
3. Use Passcode Generator on Griffin's computer
4. Escape Embassy undetected

Classified Information—Mission Overview

You must infiltrate the British Embassy in Bucharest under the strictest of conditions—you cannot employ lethal weapons at any time. Bond must use his fists, Dartgun, and brainpower to avoid detection and confrontation by the British guards and the motion-detector lasers throughout the building.

Under cover of darkness, shimmy down a rope from the glass Rotunda roof and confront as many British soldiers as you need to progress. Now venture through the Embassy's three floors. Use quiet, steady actions—remember the secret storage room for later.

Don't forget the power of unarmed combat—the only way to achieve maximum points (and respect) is for the most skilful agent to complete the entire mission using only hands as weapons.

LEGEND

Start - Start

 - Alarm Button

 - Darts

007 - 007 Bonus

Finish - Finish

British Embassy: First Floor

Be alert; as soon as you've landed at the foot of the Rotunda steps, take the Dartgun from your inventory, and run forward a couple of steps, plugging the soldier. Now run up the steps and through the double doors.

![007 Agent Under Fire logo]

Prima's Official Strategy Guide

If you venture too far up the steps or wait too long at the foot of the steps, the Embassy soldier spots you, and attempts to shoot you or raise the alarm. Subdue him before he reaches the alarm button to the right of the double doors. If the guard on the second floor spots you and runs for the alarm upstairs, your mission is over.

BEING BOND

If you have time and you're something of a sharp-shooter, take down the first guard, then immediately look up and target the guard walking along the second-floor balcony. If you don't dispatch him you'll meet him later. If you miss him, the guard usually runs out of view and raises the alarm!

TIP

For goodness sake, be careful, 007! Don't press the alarm button—covert operations are best completed without letting everyone in Bucharest know your position!

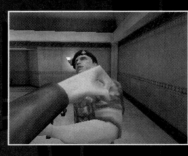

If you opt to creep slowly behind the first guard, he turns, opens the double doors, and walks into an adjoining corridor, turns left, walks a little farther, then returns to the Rotunda. Use your martial arts skills here.

Find the elevator located around the corner and to the right. Don't enter the elevator yet, though.

After the elevator, turn right and spot the guard walking away from you.

BEING BOND

The truly impressive secret agent will complete this level without any of the British soldiers knowing what is going on. Prevent the soldier from spotting Bond by waiting near the elevator, then carefully hitting the soldier as he walks into view.

Remember, if you can subdue the soldiers with just your hands, you'll get double the points!

Continue past this soldier's patrol point and enter an office. Find a trio of Darts for your Dartgun, then head back to the elevator, press the call button, and ascend.

British Embassy: Second Floor

Turn right and head down the corridor, through the double doors, and into the kitchen. You pass an alarm button on the way.

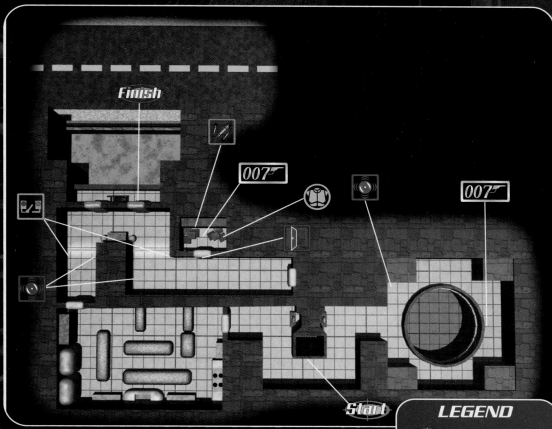

Try to traverse this room by making as little noise as possible. Unfortunately, no matter how hard you try, you brush against a bottle, cooking pot, or kitchen utensil, making a clattering noise. A guard comes to investigate.

The doors at the far end of the room open, and the guard starts to patrol. Find a hiding spot to duck behind, and remain hidden, aiming at the guard until you have a clear shot. Take it.

If you haven't engaged the guard you spotted patrolling the Rotunda balcony, turn left instead of right. Run toward the guard, take him, and then return to the kitchen.

LEGEND

Start	- Start
(icon)	- Alarm Button
(icon)	- Darts
(icon)	- Secret Door
(icon)	- Trip Wire
(icon)	- Armor
007	- 007 Bonus
Finish	- Finish

BEING BOND

If you're after a more impressive takedown, listen for the guard, wait until he turns around, and watch as he walks counterclockwise around the Rotunda balcony and confront him.

If you're spotted, the guard runs for the alarm to the left of the Rotunda entrance. Walk around the Rotunda before peering up at the guard on the third floor. A well-aimed dart takes care of him.

Alternatively, you can rush the guard. You must have a clear shot—you can't hit him through the glass of the door. React quickly to ensure that the guard doesn't raise the alarm.

In the corridor, there's a blue laser wire laid across the ground in front of you. Depending on the time and your stealth abilities, a guard may also be wandering this area. Down the guard as he walks past the windows.

Note that those with extra stealth abilities can actually nullify the laser wire. Simply equip your Q-Specs, locate the small rectangular area of wall near the wire that's a secret panel, press it, and you'll locate the wiring. Now produce your Q-Laser, and destroy the circuitry. Do this for every laser wire you see.

If you've been stealthy, crouch and edge along the wall of windows. Through the third one, you spy another guard. If you walk past the window or sneak while standing, the guard fires wildly at the window. Tag him by leaping right and firing before he has a chance to unload.

Now turn and check the rest of the corridor. Leap over the second laser wire, and round the corner. You face a dead end. Put on and activate your Q-Specs to spot a secret door in the left wall. Open the door to collect Armor and more Darts.

NOTE

Do be careful, 007. Head around the corner to incapacitate that extra guard. The door up ahead says "No Entry" for a reason—it cannot be opened. If you've stumbled into both laser wires and still haven't raised the alarm, feel free to run into them again—no more soldiers appear. It's always better to fry those circuit panels.

Head out of that open window (jump, then push through). Now on the exterior second-floor balcony, select your Q-Claw and look up. There's a mesh grill directly above you. Aim and grapple up to the third-floor balcony.

If you'd rather, run to the fire escape ladder to your left as you emerge onto the balcony and clamber up the old fashioned way.

British Embassy: Third Floor

On the third-floor balcony, run to the second open window and clamber inside. You're in a computer room, but the terminal needs a Passcode Generator to work. Continue to the room with the statue in it.

If you move directly through the statue room and turn right, you'll find a locked door—you need a Keycard n to open it. Turn back, and open the opposite door. This leads to a tiny storage room, housing three more Darts. Take these, then head back into the statue room and open the only door there.

Quickly grabbing a Keycard from a nearby desk, Bond inspects this stranger's assets. She hasn't noticed Bond's action, and seems to want her privacy....

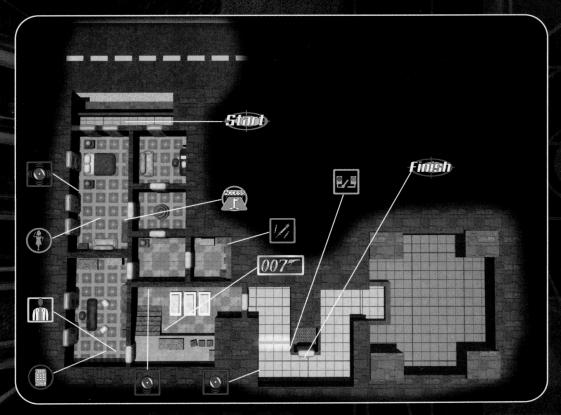

LEGEND

- **Start** - Start
- - Alarm Button
- - Darts
- - Griffin Clone
- - Trip Wire
- - Malprave
- - Keycard
- - Passcode Generator
- **007** - 007 Bonus
- **Finish** - Finish

With the Keycard in hand, return to the locked door and open it. The door swings open, revealing the secure room. There's Reginald Griffin, sitting at his desk! As Bond edges forward, he pushes Griffin's chair, and it rotates. Griffin is dead! And what's more, someone looking exactly like Griffin has you targeted with his Pistol!

The malpractices of the Identicon corporation are coming to light. Griffin's Clone must be put down, and fast. Tag the clone as quickly as possible to put him to sleep.

Griffin's Clone is quick, and determined to strike you down. If you run, he follows you all the way back to the window. The door Griffin's Clone stood in front of is locked, so take him down with haste.

Griffin's Clone drops a Passcode Generator, allowing you access to the computer in the first room on this floor. Return to the first room on this floor to receive a message from Bloch, intended for the Griffin Clone, instructing him to head for Malprave's Swiss headquarters. Your mission parameters have changed. Get out of here!

Head out of the secure room by the door Griffin's Clone stood in front of, and immediately duck down behind the chest. A guard patrols the area behind the cases of antiques. Wait until you get a clear shot (remember, Darts don't pierce glass).

Alternatively, bound down the steps, tag the guard, continue past the display cases (which can't be destroyed by the Dartgun), and round the corner.

The elevator descends back to the first floor. Once you're out, look for a British soldier to your right. If you didn't shoot him earlier in the mission, he still patrols, ready to sound the alarm. Now head left, back to the Rotunda.

Watch for the moving laser wire and the patrolling guard. Start by tagging the guard as he moves into view, and then worry about the laser wire. Jump over it on the left side, and then run around to dispatch the British soldier waiting on the third floor balcony of the Rotunda—if you haven't already taken him down. Then head back and enter the elevator.

If you trip the laser wire, prepare for a primed guard appearing in the balcony section overlooking the Rotunda, in addition to any other guards in the area.

Step through the double doors, and head straight down the steps. The exit doors directly ahead swing open, and a final guard spots you. Instantly tag him before he runs up the steps and sounds the alarm. Then head out the exit doors and into the Bucharest night.

BEING BOND

Still hoping to surprise the final guard? Run quickly to the left or right edge of the Rotunda, near the exit door, and stay low, following the guard as he walks in. Then confront him.

British Embassy: First Floor

Fancy a spot of hand-to-hand combat, 007? Then leave your Dartgun at home, and complete the entire mission by simply punching your enemy. This is the *only* way to achieve maximum points.

LEGEND

Start - Start

 - Alarm Button

Finish - Finish

MI6 Briefing

Shocking news, 007. We've conducted tests on the man who attacked you in the Embassy. He was more than just an imposter. He was an exact genetic duplicate of Griffin—in short, a clone. It seems our friend Nigel Bloch is engaged in something far more sinister than smuggling.

The message you retrieved from Griffin's computer contained the name of a company, Malprave Industries, based in Switzerland. This firm is known as a leader in bioengineering research. It fits the evidence that Malprave Industries is somehow involved in the illegal advancement of human cloning.

Your mission is to infiltrate Malprave Industries and collect any incriminating information. You'll be posing as Mr. Somerset, a journalist who has arranged an interview with Adrian Malprave, the company's owner and CEO. Once inside, look for evidence that will give us an indication of Malprave's plans.

For this mission we've provided you with your Q-Decryptor, which allows you to hack into any mainframe computer. You'll also be equipped with a micro-camera for photographing objects. In addition, you'll also be provided with a Q-Remote gadget. This clever device records electronic signals that can then be used to remotely control a matching machine or computer.

OBJECTIVES

1. Photograph Satellite Imagery
2. Photograph the Blueprints
3. Retrieve data from basement mainframes
4. Use tram cable to escape facility

Classified Information–Mission Overview

From the Alpine mountains to a cavern carved deep into the rock face, this zone requires stealth and entertaining methods of foe disposal. Once Bond realizes what's necessary to neutralize the guards without causing a firefight, you can complete this zone more easily.

Then there's the matter of collecting information by using a camera and downloading information. Follow the walkthrough to avoid needless combat, and keep cool, relying on your quieter weapons. Finally, prepare for an altercation with a couple of Malprave's seasoned shock troops before you make a trademark Bond escape.

Alpine Base–Atrium Level

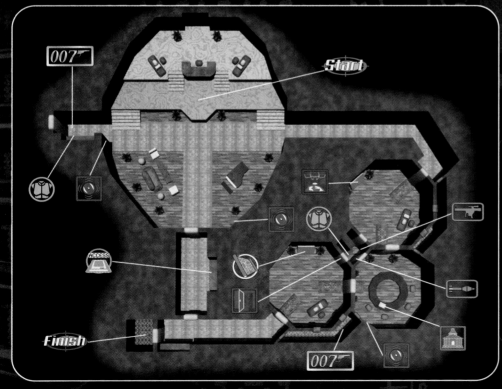

LEGEND

- **Start** - Start
- - Alarm Button
- - Secret Door
- - Building Model
- - Satellite Imagery
- **ACCESS** - Computer Access Card
- - Blueprints
- - Armor
- - MRL-22 Rocket Launcher
- - Rockets
- **007** - 007 Bonus
- **Finish** - Finish

Under the pseudonym "Mr. Somerset", Bond converses with a striking young woman called Bebe. There's another one of her–this one seems to be called Bella. They inform Bond that there's been a slight delay, and then they leave the atrium area. Bond peers up at the windows, pausing to check a stained glass window…that's Adrian Malprave! He met her at the Embassy!

A trap is about to be sprung, and Bond has nothing but a P2K and 15 minutes to escape. Bring the Pistol to bear, and then screw the silencer to the end of the barrel to help prevent combat if you tag one of Malprave's guards–the quieter the better.

You want to leave this atrium as quickly as possible. This is achieved by opening one of the doors to the right of the steps near the grand piano. But all the doors are locked.

Start by clambering up the steps to the top of the study area. At the top are three desks. Head for the one with Bella's name on it (the one to the right of the stained glass window).

BEING BOND

Now turn back to the table and locate the small green flashing button embedded in the desk. Press it.

The door to the left of the desk, at the bottom of the raised area, swings open. This is the main route out of the facility–jog down here, ignoring the two other doors.

The first one doesn't have a name attached to it–this must be Malprave's. The console button unlocks the middle door in the room, and two guards scurry out.

Take out the farthest guard first–he makes a beeline for the alarm button near the door while the other stands and fires his Shotgun. If you down the guards before the alarm sounds, you have done well.

After taking out the two guards, run through the now-open door, and check the small corridor behind it. On the bookshelf to the left is a Computer Access Card, useful later on. You can also obtain it later in this excursion. The double door at the end of the corridor is sealed.

f you move to the desk on the far right labeled "Bebe" and press the door release button, the final single door opens, and out run two guards. This only occurs if the alarm hasn't been sounded. Again, one guard stops to attack while the other tries to alert the facility by hitting the second alarm button, near this door. Tag both guards before the alarm sounds.

Run down the corridor, turning right before you come to a door and an ornate ventilation cover. The choice is yours—enter via the ventilation shaft or the door. If you're concerned about stealth, take out your Q-Laser and dissolve the lock on the hatchway to the duct.

BEING BOND

f you fail to stop the guards raising the alarm after opening either of the doors with two guards behind them, soldiers pour out of the narrow corridor near the antique couch and chairs. Attacking in squads of four, these highly organized henchmen pepper you with Shotgun and KS7 fire until you keel over. You can only stop the flood by shutting down the alarm. If you're getting swamped, back off, use the objects in the room for cover, and take down the soldiers using Shotguns.

When the melee ends (or if you open the door near the furniture and tag both guards before the alarm sounds), walk into the narrow corridor and collect the Armor if you need it. Now turn around and head to the opposite door; the double door at the end is sealed.

If you choose to crawl into the ventilation shaft that runs parallel to the rooms' exterior walls, take extreme care with your movement and aiming—if you're spotted and the alarm is raised, it will be exceptionally difficult to fight in these cramped quarters. Move to the first grill, look through at the guard, and subdue him.

Now move to the corner, wait until the soldier in the adjacent room moves out of sight, then advance to the second grating, looking out onto the first room again. Wait until a second guard opens the doors leading from the first to the second room, then take him down.

At this point, you can either laser your way into this room, or turn around, wait for the third guard to stroll by the third grating, and plug him before he spots you—usually as he walks past the large maps on the far side of the table.

BEING BOND

CONTINUED

Now laser the lock off the grating and move into the second chamber.

If at any time the alarm is sounded, groups of two to four guards burst into the central room from either exit. Turn the alarm off and guard it to prevent more reinforcements from appearing. Failure to switch the alarm off results in countless enemies, who eventually whittle down your armor.

When the coast is clear, head to the table and inspect the Building Model sitting on it. Produce your Q-Camera and snap away. When you've taken a quality photograph, exit through the doors to the left of the glass window with the Rocket Launcher in it.

 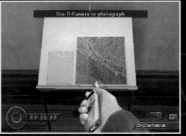

If you want to stand and take down your man, open the door to the initial room, and carefully aim at the guard looking at the large picture of Bella (or is it Bebe?). Pocket the guard's weapon, then check the room. To the right of the painting is an easel, and resting on the easel are Satellite Imagery Documents. Use your Q-Camera to photograph the folder and map.

If you wish, you can smash the glass to obtain the Rocket Launcher. However, this isn't wise, and sets off the alarm. Grab the weapon, sprint back and turn off the alarm, and deal with any remaining soldiers.

In the second room, you have just enough time to take down the second guard before he spots you. If he reacts or you miss, he runs to the alarm on the wall between the two sets of maps. Tag the enemy.

BEING BOND

There's one more room to infiltrate in this area. A cunning secret agent will laser the lock of the grating to the left of the door, crawl in, and move to one of the two gratings facing the third chamber. From here, aim and take down the patrolling guard, then enter the room.

Seconds later, the third guard appears from the double doors leading to a third chamber. Perform the same action, guarding the alarm button (there is only one in this area), and shooting the fellow immediately. Repeat this once more with the fourth guard.

Otherwise, enter through the door, run into the room, and either wait for the guard to enter the room, or dispatch him if he's already there. Then make a quick checklist: Have you taken photos of the Satellite Imagery and the Blueprints (next to the secret door)? Good.

BEING BOND

If you didn't smash the glass in front of the Rocket Launcher, move to the painting of Bella and hit the action button. A secret door slides back, allowing you access to Armor and the weapon without raising the alarm.

If you haven't picked up the Computer Access Card yet, don't head for the elevator. Instead, open the double doors near the guard you just took out, and check the right-hand bookcase. The card is nestled there. The far double doors lead back to the atrium. Now head back to the elevator.

Alpine Base-Basement Level

Exit through the far door, run down the passage, and halt just before the corner. There's a final guard to nix. Wait until the guard starts to patrol, then tag him.

If you reached the elevator with time to spare, M lets you know. If you didn't reach the elevator in time, then you must inspect the atrium again! Step out of the elevator and immediately dispatch the guard. He must not reach the alarm in front of him!

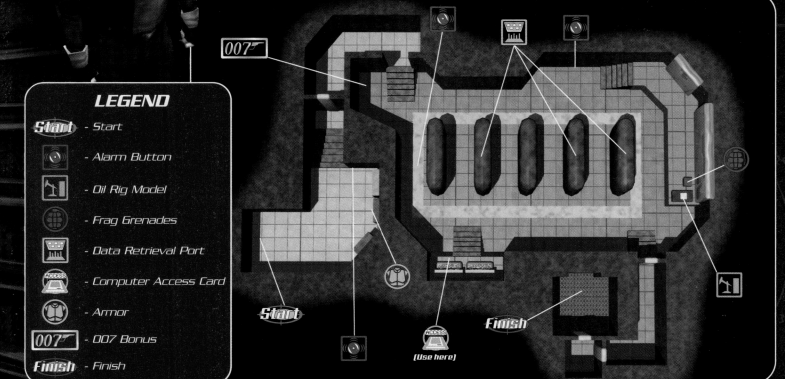

LEGEND

- **Start** - Start
- (icon) - Alarm Button
- (icon) - Oil Rig Model
- (icon) - Frag Grenades
- (icon) - Data Retrieval Port
- (icon) - Computer Access Card
- (icon) - Armor
- **007** - 007 Bonus
- **Finish** - Finish

Did he reach the alarm in front of him? Now you'll have to contend with two to four more guards attacking from the bottom of the stairs. Venture down the steps, then return to the elevator. Guards appear here as well, if the alarm isn't silenced. Shut it off, then head down the steps.

If you're quick, run down the steps, sidestep left, head down between the second and third computer bank, and tag the guard. This only occurs if you haven't raised the alarm.

Now run to the far side of the computer banks and up toward the windows. Turn left to see the second guard strolling along the opposite side. (If you were slow, he may be between the two far computer banks.) Take him down.

TIP

If the alarm sounds at any time during your infiltration of this area, two guards rush in from the elevator area, and down the steps, attempting to gun you down. Switch off the alarm, and then tackle your foes, or you'll find the supply seems to be limitless.

With all enemies disposed of, run to the computer terminal in one corner of the room, and insert your Computer Access Card. The display should read "Data Port Alarms Disabled." Excellent news—now you can use your Q-Decryptor to download the computer information.

It's time to download all available data. Head to the second computer bank, flick on your Q-Decryptor, and commence the download. Now move to the fourth bank and repeat the process. The fifth bank houses the last pieces of information. Objective complete.

TIP

Didn't find the Computer Access Card? Then every time you download information from the Data Ports, an alarm sounds and you face two or more soldiers. Switch off the alarm, tackle the remaining enemies, and repeat the process.

The final part of this sortie, prior to your escape, is to photograph the one remaining Building Model located on a shallow gantry near the fifth computer bank. Step onto the platform, move around, and snap that shot. Then look at the open box at your feet. It contains three Frag Grenades. Pick them up, then down the two incoming guards.

When you've completed the downloads and taken the photographs, the electronic lock on the secure door near the fifth computer bank activates. Run to the door and press the lock to open it. Then run down the corridor, open the second secure door, step onto the elevator, and activate it.

Alpine Base-Caverns

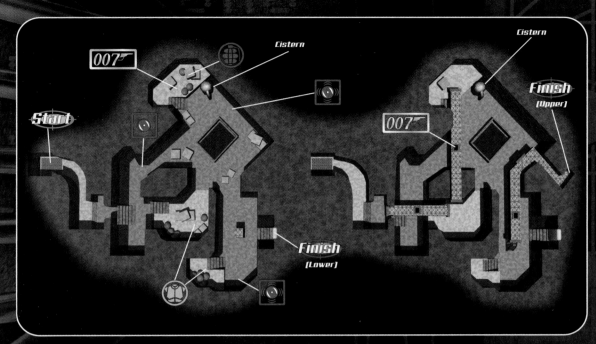

Cistern

007

Cistern

Start

Finish
[Upper]

007

Finish
[Lower]

LEGEND

Start - Start

- Ammunition

- Alarm Button

- Frag Grenades

- Q-Remote Transmitter

- Door Program

- Armor

007 - 007 Bonus

Finish - Finish

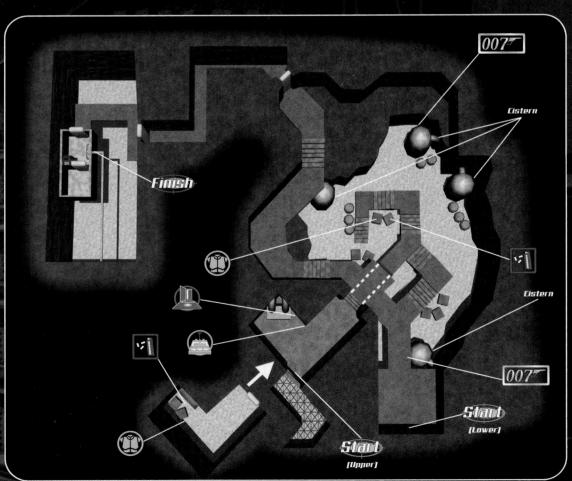

007

Cistern

Finish

Cistern

Cistern

007

Start
[Lower]

Start
[Upper]

As the elevator descends, inspect the weapons you've picked up from recently departed guards. Arm yourself with the silenced P2K. Run around the platform to the secure door, and either open it or Q-Claw up to the duct.

BEING BOND

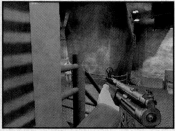 

Duck on the other side of the door. Turn left to see three guards patrolling. Aim at the first one (while crouching), and peg him with a well-aimed shot. Now creep down the steps and take down the second guard from range.

Alternatively, you can strike the second and third guards if you quickly run down the set second of steps to the lowered alcove, and aim at both guards as they walk past. Silenced weapons only, please! And don't forget to pick up the Armor!

Another option is to run into the main area, tagging the remaining two guards. That's three guards down and no one the wiser. Good work, 007—now move to the open hatch in the duct, near the green pit.

You can follow a similar plan of action if you arm yourself with the Frinesi (Shotgun) or the Defender. Open the door, run at your victim, firing once at close range, and repeat two times for quick results.

An alternative and sneakier plan involves zipping up to the duct, crawling across the main walkway, and dropping into the storage bay. From there, Q-Claw to the next duct and crawl to the end of it. On the way,

you can look out at another duct—this one leading to a very important area. Don't cut the locks though—you can fall and become a target. A grated vantage point is an excellent spot to take guards out with a silenced pistol.

If the enemy sounds the alarm, expect reinforcements from behind you (the secure door where you came from), and alert guards in the second area with the boxes and the blast door.

BEING BOND

If you prefer silent takedowns, and you've reached the third open duct, use the Q-Claw to lift yourself into the duct, turn left, and continue down the duct until you reach the orange-lit antechamber. Carefully edge forward, then point your Defender down and around to the left, tagging the guard before he sees you.

If you crave action instead, head down toward the blast door, watching out for the guard patrolling the far end. If he spots you, another guard from the room behind the open blast door attempts to close it, blocking your way. Use the crates, and duck to prevent this plan from going horribly wrong.

You can also enter the ducts by ladder, on the far side of the main duct near the blast door. Don't forget the second lowered alcove with more barrels and Armor. Shimmy up when the coast is clear, and continue until you reach the orange-lit antechamber.

You can enter the cavernous room via the blast door, or by the ducts. If you move through the blast door, carefully aim at the sniper soldier on the platform ahead, or rush him and Shotgun him as he attempts to change weapons.

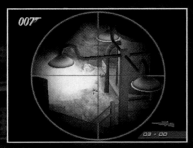

With the newly acquired SSR 4000, move to the end of the platform and check the winding metal steps below. At the bottom, two guards wait patiently. Instead of tagging them, you can target a barrel and six nearby casks detonate simultaneously, or else fire at the valve handle next to either soldier, releasing hot steam and incapacitating the henchmen. The choice is yours.

Now go down the steps to the second level, and turn left. Notice the orange-lit room and the enemy firing at you. Retaliate, and then enter this area.

Note the end of the duct where those who chose the stealthier option would've entered.

BEING BOND

There are many devastating ambush tactics to try in this area. For a start, before venturing to the orange-lit room, head back toward the blast doors, turn around, hug the left wall, and drop onto the three barrels. Walk forward and fire a single devastating salvo at the guard that runs out of the ground-level room.

He has a chum who either follows him out or stays behind and fires at you. Once departed, pick up the guards' weapons, try on the Armor, and take the extra Ammunition in this small red-lit room.

Another option is to run all the way down the steps, scoot behind the boxes at the bottom, and wait for the two guards to run out. Take up a location near two more steam valves, and then plug the valve, the barrels, or the guards themselves with any weapon you want. Grenades are particularly appropriate.

Back at the orange-lit room, you'll see a lock mechanism that you must use your Q-Remote on to exit the room. Activate the Q-Remote, and the data is transferred.

after Shotgun blast at him, side-stepping out of the corner, then back into cover until he moves.

Another way to inflict a little damage before the combat starts is to lob a couple of Frag Grenades around the corner, and then charge in with your Shotgun blazing. Once combat is complete, return to the cavern to claim any Armor you left.

Now move out of the orange-lit room. If you haven't entered the cavernous room yet, take out the guards from the balcony you start on, then turn around and tag the sniper guard behind you. After you secure the area, head up to the top of the steps, turn right, and follow the upper platform all the way to the exit door.

If the door lock is emanating green light, your Q-Remote has successfully taken the door-locking data from the control panel. If not, head back to the orange-lit room and transfer the information. Open the door and step through.

Take care, 007—around the next corner lurk two of Malprave's cloned Berserker Soldiers! Carrying a Frinesi Shotgun, he immediately fires at you! Retaliate with Shotgun blasts until he falls, backing up as the fight progresses.

After the fracas, head around the corner, and Shotgun the waiting guard at the cable car entrance. One guard remains—a Sniper-Rifle carrying enemy, intent on shooting you as you approach this level's exit.

Load up with the Defender, sidle through the door, and plug the Sniper-Rifle guard with one shot. Otherwise, you'll have to turn right, run around the gangplank to the cable car control, and take down the guard from the shelter of the control room. Single-shot weapons and Frag Grenades work well if your aim is true.

In the control room, find the ladder near the opposite door, and climb up to the roof of the room. From here, move toward the cable car hook and grab it with ■. Moments later, Bond is riding the cable car wire out of Malprave's Alpine Base for good. Well done, 007!

BEING BOND

Once the first Berserker is down, duck and move to the corner, then slowly peek around until you spot the second Berserker Soldier. Let off a Defender round to get a free hit, and then plant Shotgun blast

MI6 Briefing

The data you retrieved in Switzerland included a file titled "damaged goods." We believe this is a code word for Dr. Natalya Damescu, who used to work for Malprave. Dr. Damescu recently fled Switzerland and returned to her homeland, Romania.

007, Dr. Damescu fled with a Data Chip containing information on something known as "Poseidon." Fearing for her life, Dr. Damescu has taken refuge in the British Embassy in Bucharest.

We think Malprave has hired Carla the Jackal to raid the Embassy and kidnap Dr. Damescu. Bond, you must prevent Dr. Damescu from being kidnapped at all costs!

Q-Branch has a safehouse located in an upper-floor apartment around the corner from the Embassy. Look for a sho street with a tree. You'll need your Q-Claw gadget to gain access to the safehouse balcony. R is there to provide you wi a device that will let you infiltrate the Embassy.

OBJECTIVES

1. Use Q-Claw to enter R's safehouse
2. Infiltrate Embassy
3. Rescue 5 civilian hostages
4. Find secret passage and rescue Dr. Natalya Damescu
5. Destroy helicopter gunship

Classified Information–Mission Overview

The enemy forces of Malprave have launched an all-out offensive against our British boys, and the consulate is being attacked. Quickly dispatch these invaders–the lives of your countrymen are once again at stake! The fraught combat moves from the streets to a narrow alley, where seeking cover is the best plan.

Following this, a brief Q-Clawing expedition over the rooftops ends with an anti-climax, so to speak, and an audience with R. Then it's on to the interior of the Embassy. Take care to shoot enemies in combat fatigues, and not Embassy personnel. After this, locate the secret door, run to the elevator, and head into combat with Carla the Jackal.

Finally, you make it onto the roof just in time to spot a helicopter leaving, and another, more heavily armored helicopter ascending into view. Now comes a firefight with a gunship, where swift moving and constant targeting of the enemy are imperative. Only by facing these enemies can you rescue Dr. Damescu.

British Embassy Exterior–Night

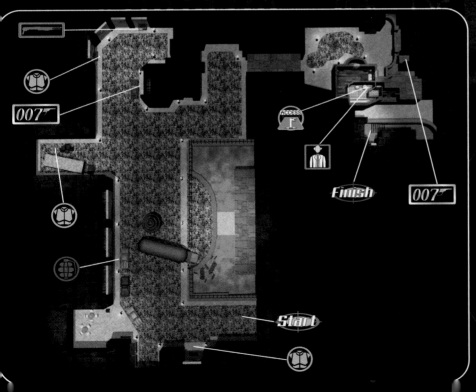

LEGEND

Start	– Start
(R figure)	– R
ACCESS	– Keycard
(grenade icon)	– Frag Grenades
(armor icon)	– Armor
(shotgun icon)	– Frinesi Shotgun
007	– 007 Bonus
Finish	– Finish

30

Bond starts this mission in an alleyway next to the British Embassy, and as soon as you take a couple of steps forward, an armored bus hurtles along the street to your left and rams the front gate. Terrorists pour out and attempt to shoot their way into the consulate!

Start by affixing the silencer to the tip of your P2K. Now move forward, heading directly for the building with the porch containing the two planters. Prepare for combat.

NOTE

Simply running around the corner, past the bus, and attempting to take on as many terrorists as possible is *not* the preferred strategy of a secret agent.

After running to the left end of the porch and hiding behind the planters, stay alert and tag the two enemies that run in from around the corner. Fire three shots from your P2K into each one to make them fall. When combat is over, quickly move to their bodies and procure the KA-57 Machine Gun. Keep this weapon holstered for the moment.

Move forward to the euro-style cars parked against the curb, and sidestep left until you spot a terrorist kneeling behind the third car. Be extremely careful—this enemy carries Grenades, and he's not afraid to throw them! If you hear the sound of a Grenade hitting sidewalk, retreat immediately, then run in and finish the guard with three P2K shots.

This leaves only the two guards roaming the fountain area in the middle of the cobblestone plaza. As you take out the Grenadier, both guards turn and spot you. Use the final bullets in your P2K to down them. The guards may run around the fountain; either stay in this area and aim from the cover of the car, or simply wade in and tag them.

BEING BOND

Pick up all the weapons and ammo the enemies drop. Grab the four Grenades behind the third small car, and a Viper weapon with a powerful six-shot capacity.

With the first five opponents vanquished, turn your attention to the red laser beam emanating from the street to your left. The beam comes from a sniper aiming at the nearby Embassy. If you stay near the wall, then aim up and leap out with your Machine Gun, you can take out the guard before he has a chance to target you. If you take too long or simply walk out into the open, you'll be badly damaged by a sniper shot.

When the sniper falls out of view, run up the small alley where a damaged truck and a load of crates block your path. Among the crates, near the gated alley and locked door, is Armor. Take it—you probably took damage in the preceding fight.

NOTE

Don't get too close to the coach the enemy used to ram the gates—it explodes about 30 seconds into the mission. And don't try to enter the gated courtyard—the gates are impenetrable, and the coach blocks your path.

BEING BOND

Before you attempt to locate the secret entrance to the Embassy, down the four terrorists who are attacking the front of the Embassy. Start by loading your Viper, and edge to the fenced perimeter. All four enemies are firing at the building, and they won't notice you until you start tagging them, so make that aim count!

Start by either throwing in a Grenade (remember your elevation—we don't want that Grenade bouncing off the fence and into your hands!), then switching to the Machine Gun or Viper.

Alternatively, target one of the enemies, and take him down with one shot. If you don't mind taking a bit of damage, aim for the remaining three guards—you'll save ammo. Otherwise, you need two Viper shots per guard.

Good work, 007: Now to find the side entrance to the Embassy. M chimes in with further information, but don't head directly around the perimeter yet—continue along the main road to the alleyway where the single car is parked, and check the shop windows.

NOTE

In this alley, find the window above the park bench, smash it with a single bullet, and don the Armor inside after you leap up into the display. You'll also find a shotgun in an adjacent window.

Now move back, go around the perimeter, and head for the arched alleyway to the left of the Embassy. As you near the alley, a guard runs out to meet you. Greet him with Machine Gun fire, and then quickly move into the alleyway.

As you pass through the alley, two more guards appear—one from the courtyard near the tree, and the other from a side door to the right. With Machine Gun at the ready, dispatch both of the guards, and then run into the courtyard.

By now, you should have spotted the red laser of a second sniper in front of you. He's perched on a high balcony, and you must approach with extreme care. Line up the shot by locating the balcony the sniper is on, then sidestep from cover to behind the tree. Pop your head out, shoot, then return to the tree. Keep firing until the sniper's laser disappears–this shows he's fallen down on the job.

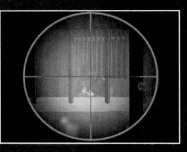

Note that you can simply run through the initial stages of this level, bypassing all the enemies, into the side alley, and then take down the sniper from his nest. Now you can retrace your steps plugging away with sniper fire. Fun, but difficult to accomplish–and you'll need those bullets for later!

Now run to the far end of the alleyway. Gah! All of the doors are locked! Just where is this rendezvous point with R? Look up to see a metal grating on the building to the right of the sniper's nest.

Your Q-Claw should already be selected in your inventory. Simply aim your target at the mesh, fire the Q-Claw, and launch yourself up onto the narrow balcony. From there, look around.

To your left is a second story bedroom with a fan and a locked window. You could smash this…but first, leap from the balcony to the sniper's area and pick up the Rifle he left behind. There's another mesh to Q-Claw to afterwards.

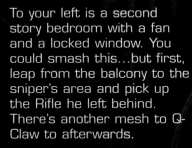

Now enter the bedroom. Smash the side window with a single bullet, leap up, and clamber through. The other option is to follow the balcony around to the double doors, one of which has conveniently been left open. This is the preferred route. Look around the room, then move to the small corridor with the two doors.

The door to the right is firmly locked, and no amount of budging can open it. This leaves you with the left door. Open it, and you stumble on the Romanian occupant's bathroom. She's taking a shower.

Enter the bathroom, heading for the shower. It suddenly descends, revealing R's not-so-lithe form. He gives you a Keycard that acts as a skeleton key. When the briefing is over, the shower ascends, allowing you to exit via a secret balcony.

Ignore the potted plants and focus on the mesh plate on the wall in front of you. Q-Claw your way to the side-entrance, drop down, and then drop again to ground level. Ignore the iron gate—it is firmly locked—and instead go under the arched entrance and locate the

Embassy side door. Press the lock to the left of the door, opening the entrance and allowing you into the Embassy.

British Embassy Interior-Night

Inside the consulate, move around the door and collect the suit of Armor in the alcove underneath the steps. Then continue up the stairs until you reach the door directly above the entrance. Head through.

On the other side of the door, a woman shrieks, and runs out of an opposite room, followed by a terrorist. Remember—shoot the enemy, not the civilian!

The room behind the guard houses nothing of interest. Turn your attention to the corridor to the left. Walk down it, then swing left and take out the guard to the left. He drops an Ingalls Machine Gun, which can be used from now on. Don't hit the civilians! The room to the right is of no interest.

From the second enemy you tagged, wander past the overturned furniture, but don't check the door to your left. Instead, sneak up to the window and train your sights on one of the two guards roughing up the hostages.

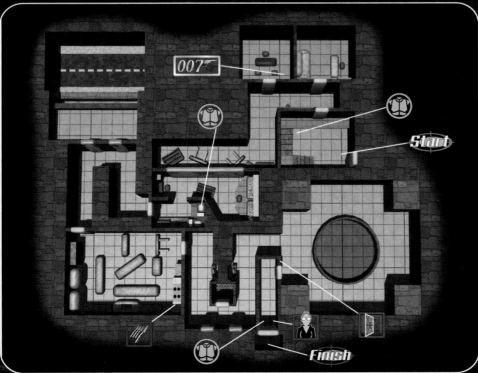

LEGEND

Start	- Start
	- Secret "Union Jack" Door
	- Sniper Rifle Ammunition
	- Dr. Damescu
	- Armor
007	- 007 Bonus
Finish	- Finish

These windows are break-able. Train a Machine Gun on one of the enemies, and let rip. When one guard falls, turn and fire at the second one. The hostages drop to their knees, allowing you to engage the enemies with ease.

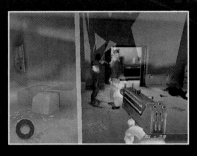

Head down the corridor and into the kitchens. Don't bother aiming at the guards from behind the doors; the bullets don't pass through the glass. Quickly run through the kitchen and arm yourself with the Machine Gun, run to the corner, open fire on the two guards, run to the next corner, and finish the two other guards.

Stay on the same side as the corridor, there's another enemy lurking behind the door you walked past. Turn and fire at him until he yields, then leap onto the windowsill, down into the room, and head for the doorway. Collect the dropped weapons!

Go through the rear door into an electrical switch room. Pick up the armor that's hidden behind the machine to your left and then carry on through the new door to the right.

You're back in familiar territory. Head right down the corridor, and then turn left. Hold steady for a moment; as you walk past the two orange vases, the far window on the right explodes. Through the wreckage of the window, a Special Forces guard seems

intent on lobbing a Grenade at you. Cut him down before he can throw it.

BEING BOND

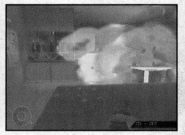

Halt the four guards on kitchen detail by opening the doors, lobbing a Grenade at the guard behind the shelving in front of you, and then retreating. Repeat this process with the remaining guards, but be careful about the Grenades bouncing back!

Alternatively, swing the doors open and snipe all four guards from the entrance. You'll bewilder them and take less damage than a run through with guns.

BEING BOND

After throwing a Grenade, the soldier draws a Pistol and shoots at you from cover. Engage him with Machine Gun fire, or use the Sniper Rifle to tag him from a distance.

Through the kitchen exit, head into a second corridor, turning right and then left. Beware! There are two extremely proficient guards on Bond-elimination detail just around the corner from the elevator.

CAUTION

Don't call the elevator—that thick smoke billowing from the elevator shaft damages you if you attempt to board the elevator.

As soon as you venture past the elevator, two guards attempt to shoot you, and these guys are more professional than the chaps you encountered before. Backtrack, dropping Grenades in their path or firing at them with your Machine Gun as they chase you.

Around the final corner, you almost run into one last guard at the entrance to the Rotunda. Tag him before he opens fire. Now in the Rotunda, listen to M's message.

There's a hidden door somewhere in this area. There wasn't one when you checked this area in the initial Embassy infiltration, but now it has been activated. It's behind the Union Jack (the flag of the United Kingdom).

Run down the narrow corridor, take the Armor to the right of the service elevator, and meet up with Dr. Damescu. She informs you that the Data Chip containing the information on Poseidon has been stolen. Now swipe the Keycard and wait for the lift to descend—you have a meeting with Carla the Jackal!

British Embassy Rooftop–Night

LEGEND

Start	- Start
	- Ingalls Ammuntion
	- Viper Ammunition
	- Carla the Jackal
	- Armor
	- MRL-22 Rocket Launcher
	- Rockets
	- Ingalls
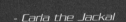	- FSU-4
007	- 007 Bonus
Finish	- Finish

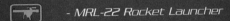

As the elevator ascends, move to the right side of it and train your weapon slightly diagonally upwards. As soon as the doors open, take out the enemy that ambushes you on a balcony–hit him or the barrels behind him for a spectacular takedown. If you're after more Armor and ammunition, explode the barrels underneath the balcony and collect the items.

When the coast is clear and the Armor and ammo collected, head straight through the set of double doors opposite your location, and into the building's main air-conditioning room. Carla the Jackal is waiting for you!

Defeating Carla the Jackal

Carla may be a jackal, but she's also a sly fox, using the balcony to gain a significant height advantage. She attacks using a Windsor Machine Gun with an optional Grenade Launcher attachment. What does this mean? Severe pain for those who don't like to hide behind crates.

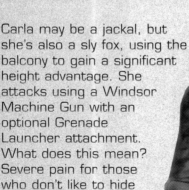

Carla lobs Grenades at you if you're in the open, otherwise utilizing the Machine Gun and blasting you or the crates you're hiding behind. Check her location, aim up, and fight back!

Start by running to the set of boxes straight in front of you. They're stacked high, and provide a decent amount of cover. But beware; after about 15 seconds of fire, the top boxes explode, leaving you exposed. Move forward into cover–Carla loves to lob Grenades in here. Sidestepping out from a wall and then retreating back behind it also works well.

Thwart Carla by firing either a constant stream of Machine Gun bullets, or by hitting her with four or five Viper shots. Fire once or twice, then sidestep into cover. Continue until Carla retreats into a corner.

The corner of the balcony houses a group of barrels. When Carla is next to them, fire at the barrels to hit her with collateral damage, and run to the middle of the far section of balcony.

It only takes three more Viper shots on target for her to realize you mean business. She scampers behind a thick metal gate. Don't move from the area behind the boxes unless you want a Grenade to the face.

When Carla is behind the thick metal gate, she's impervious to Machine Gun fire, and difficult to hit with the Viper. Bring out the Sniper Rifle. Aim from behind the boxes and blast away two or three times.

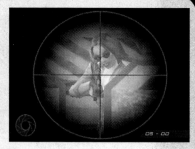

If you wish to dispose of Carla in a more appropriate manner, run to the right side of the room to the crates stacked near a large ventilation duct. Next to the crates is a metal pole with a button. Press it.

The metal gates open, and Carla is pushed off the balcony by a large metal arm. She plummets into the ventilation duct, meeting an untimely end.

Once the fight is over, climb up the ladder to the left of the room, and head around the balcony. Don't inspect the duct too closely—you don't want to follow Carla's lead.

As you step onto the area with the metal arm, pick up Carla's Windsor and the Armor at the end of the walkway. Now enter the door on the exterior wall, just after the crane arm. It leads up a short flight of steps.

After another door, you appear on the rooftops just in time to see a civilian helicopter leave the helipad. Curses! But what's that other whirring sound? Sounds like a military helicopter....

Helicopter Gunship Battle

Quickly turn your attention to the right side of the rooftop—a huge gunship bristling with Machine Guns and Rockets is ascending with a single purpose—the destruction of a certain secret agent.

It's going to be difficult taking down this brute without losing a few Armor points—or limbs. Run to the Sentry Gun on the right side of the building, near the entrance door.

You're behind partial cover—use this to your advantage, and blast away at the helicopter until the gun's ammunition runs out. Then run to the other side of the building, locate a second Sentry Gun, and repeat the process.

Whenever the gunship attempts to launch Rockets, either grin and bear it or detach yourself from the Sentry Gun and run out of the way to prevent further damage. Alternatively, you can shoot the Rockets out of the air with your gun—difficult, but not impossible.

Helicopter Gunship Battle
Continued

After you unload with the initial two Sentry Guns, try hitting the gunship with Rockets from the Rocket Launcher on the left-hand corner of the roof, or try the Windsor's Machine-guns. Grab Armor from behind the crates on the left-hand side.

For a safer option, run to either of the two Sentry Guns at the far end of the roof and continue blasting. If you hit with all your Sentry Gun bullets, you'll destroy the gunship after you've appropriated the third Sentry Gun. Experts prefer to grab their

Sniper Rifle and accurately plant a shot into the gunship pilot.

The gunship ascends from the right and swings to the left, descending out of view. Then it reappears and continues to move above you, launching Rockets after around 15 seconds of fire. Stay in one Sentry Gun place until the ammunition runs out—don't run for a nearer Sentry Gun—this allows the helicopter to hit you.

When the gunship is weakened, Rockets are also effective (aim and fire fast, or you'll be shot)—there are more Rockets to collect in the middle of the front of the building. Only use Rockets when the gunship is smoking from Sentry Gun fire.

Don't run around the helipad, try to hit the gunship with Machine Guns, or attempt to dodge the bullets it fires. Supplement your fire with portable weapons like the FSU-4 or the rocket launcher.

You know you've finished off the gunship when it starts to spin out of control, slowly tumbling toward the near side of the building. As the helicopter starts to rotate and belch smoke, run to the far edge of the rooftop and watch the gunship smash into the Embassy buildsing

you just stepped out of. If you decided to wait by the building, you find a couple of tons of twisted metal falling your way—so best to move out of the way!

After you destroy the gunship, prepare for a race through the Romanian night to reclaim that Data Chip....

MI6 Briefing

In her debriefing, Dr. Damescu informed us that Poseidon is a secret laboratory where Malprave develops her clone replicants. However, Poseidon's location remains a mystery–that information was on the Data Chip stolen by Carla's henchmen.

Dr. Damescu installed a micro-beacon on the Data Chip, but it requires a special locator to read its signal. R has delivered a suitable tracking device to the local train station for your immediate retrieval.

Our satellite reconnaissance indicates that the helicopter pilot jettisoned the chip somewhere over the city before his damaged craft was destroyed. Malprave's men will undoubtedly be looking for it, so you must recover it as quickly as possible.

Once you have the Chip, you'll need to deliver it to R's field office on the other side of the river. R's analysis should reveal the location of Poseidon.

OBJECTIVES

1. Retrieve Q-Locator
2. Locate Data Chip
3. Deliver Data Chip to R

Classified Information–Mission Overview

Time to test out Mr. Bond's most famous Q-tweaked roadster, the Aston Martin DB5. This classic has upgraded enhancements.

Using the map and following the radar is imperative in this mission, because it is easy to get lost in the narrow cobbled streets of Bucharest. Follow the directions here, and don't take a wrong turn.

Bond appropriates a battle tank on his way to deliver a Data Chip to R–now is the time to make the most of the Chain Gun, and learn each enemy's movements–especially when they come into view. With judicious use of the tank cannon in the final confrontation (to take out a train, not a tank), Bond can save the day again.

Streets of Bucharest–Night

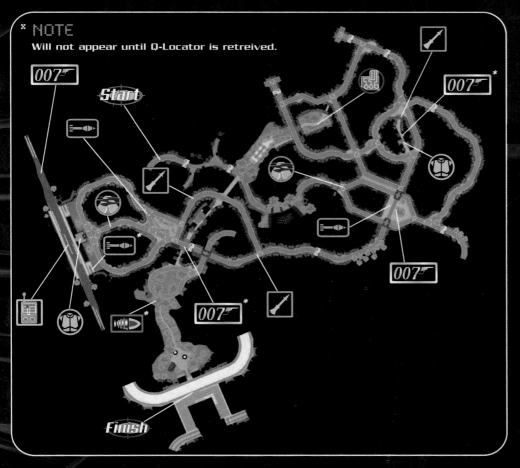

* NOTE
Will not appear until Q-Locator is retreived.

LEGEND

Start	- Start
	- Armor
007	- 007 Bonus
	- Ch-6 Mini Rockets
	- Missiles
	- Q-Locator
	- Q-Slick
	- Q-Booster
	- Data Chip
Finish	- Finish

Bond's nighttime escapade can be approached in a number of ways—the roadway has numerous junctions for you to negotiate as you search for the Q-Locator. The following information provides the fastest route to collect the Locator and the Data Chip.

From your starting position, follow the road as it snakes through a medieval church and cobbled streets. Proceed down the hill, checking ahead for a sedan.

The car weaving manically houses a henchman peeping out of the sunroof brandishing a Machine Gun at you. Use Machine Gun fire to line up a couple of Rockets to halt this threat.

At the bottom of the hill lies the Q-Slick power-up. Don't use it yet—keep your Rockets primed at the enemy. When you hit the Y-junction in the road, take either route as the road joins up again soon.

BEING BOND

To scream through this level at a breakneck pace and score the highest points possible, use the sidewalks or pavements at every opportunity—if a road is snaking uphill, steer your car in a straight line up it, usually onto pavement. Avoid obstacles (these include lamps and fire hydrants)—if you hit an obstacle you'll slow slightly, but you won't damage the car.

As the roads from the Y-junction merge back into one, a limousine with a sunroof henchman armed with a Machine Gun pulls out in front of you, weaving and attempting to slow you down. Three Rocket strikes (or two and then Machine Gun fire) takes out the limo.

TIP

When firing Rockets, launch them where the limo is going, not at its current location. You want your Rocket to hit as the limo turns a corner, so aim slightly to one side when approaching a corner.

Once you've demolished the limo, weave to the top of the hill, avoiding lampposts. When you pass under the bridge, there are three routes to take—one straight ahead blocked by limos, one to the left, and the preferred shorter route through an archway. Aim directly for the Missile power-up, and head through this archway.

As you rattle down this narrow alleyway, run over the Armor power-up. When the road widens, head toward for the bridge. You're about to encounter another enemy vehicle.

There's a park on your right down the road. As soon as you see the park, swerve right and cut diagonally across it to collect the crate of Rockets. If Rockets aren't your bag, stay on the left road.

As you near the bridge, an armored van cuts in front of you and a shutter opens, revealing a henchman armed with a Rocket Launcher. Fire off three Rockets in quick succession to stop the van in its tracks. This should occur before you drive over the bridge, and claim more Rockets.

Taking the road just ahead of the Rockets, weave as it curves, until you spot the elaborate train station. You can head straight through the gap to the right (left of the main entrance), or straight through the entrance, picking up the Armor and swerving right.

As you enter another downhill stretch just past the bridge, two more sedans join in the fun; one in front of you, the other behind. Dispatch the one in front with two Rockets, two Missiles, or constant Machine Gun fire (or a combination of the three—although Rockets are recommended). To stop the other car, change to Q-Slick and pour it behind you.

BEING BOND

There's nothing as satisfying as spotting an enemy vehicle lurching through a puddle of Q-Slick in your rearview mirror. To ambush your opponent, spill your fluids at a corner in the road, where the enemy is most likely to run over it.

Feeling the need to detonate every enemy vehicle in this mission? Then switch to Missiles as you near the train station, and launch two at the helicopter hovering over the tracks. Then tag the second helicopter as you collect the Q-Locator. You'll be rewarded with Bond Move points.

As soon as you pass the cross-street on your right, another limo will pull out in front of you; the sunroof enemy is equipped with a rocket launcher, so it's imperative you subdue him as quickly as possible. Switch to your missiles, and fire off two in quick succession. This should deal with him accordingly.

As you wrench your car right, enter the platform and swerve onto the tracks. Now head across the tracks, and around the front of the far train (there's a small gap between the train and the wall).

Now on the other side of the station, head down the second platform, aiming your vehicle at the Q-Locator in the middle of the road. Pick it up immediately!

The preferred plan (as there's little spare time to stop and battle a helicopter) is to simply speed up and weave left and right to avoid its fire until it gives up the chase.

After five seconds of locating, the Data Chip's location is displayed on the HUD map. Swerve around the trains and out of the train station through the right-hand exit.

While you're dealing with this airborne menace, a sedan with a Rocket-packing enemy spruces up the proceedings. At the summit of the hill, deploy a Q-Slick to leave the sedan floundering. Otherwise, ignore this enemy; he calls off the pursuit shortly.

Now back on the roadway, a van housing a henchman with a Rocket Launcher roars in from the left. Quickly change to your Missiles, and launch a well-timed shot at the van. With it dispatched, return to the route you took to the train station.

Through an archway, a roving helicopter fires a devastating salvo of Rockets at the bridge ahead, destroying it as you accelerate to cross it. Ignore the helicopter and the inferno, and floor the accelerator, jumping clean over the fiery gap. Points are duly awarded.

The roads of Bucharest are narrow and bordered by tall buildings, so Missiles are more likely to hit scenery than enemy vehicles if your timing is off. Launch Missiles only when you aren't near a bridge or directly in front of a lamppost.

After the leap, follow the arrow on the HUD map up the road, and watch for a van zooming in from the left. Immediately launch two Missiles to total it, and then concentrate on the road ahead.

Your next adversary is a limousine with a sunroof henchman. Speedily take out the limo; any connecting projectiles can spell doom for your battered Aston Martin. Rockets or Missiles work extremely well here.

Keep the pedal to the metal while approaching the first intersection. A helicopter shoots at you. If you have the skill, hit it with a Missile as soon as it appears, then slow and tag it as it flies overhead.

As you near a junction, make a sharp left and head uphill toward an archway on the left corner of the road. Failure to make the left return results in you ploughing into a locked gate and losing valuable time.

Approaching the archway, the green blip on the radar shows the exact location of the Data Chip. Once through the archway, you appear in an enclosed park with the chip in the middle of the pavement. Run over it!

Collect the Q-Booster at the entrance to the courtyard walkway–this is vital to completing the level. If you miss the Q-Booster, there are two more hidden in the park ahead–one on each side.

With the Data Chip in your possession, the timer resets. Head directly for the archway at the opposite end of the park, and watch as two sedans pull out in front of you, blocking the exit. Should you ram through them? That's one possibility.

Switch to the Q-Booster at once, and continue to floor the accelerator. Zoom down the paved path and keep in the center to avoid the helicopter's continuing assault. Prepare for a dangerous maneuver!

BEING BOND

Ramming the sedans or firing at them isn't going to win you any kudos. Hitting the sandwich board under the arch, knocking your car up onto two wheels, and then passing through the gap between the cars without firing a single shot, however, is. Aim slightly to the right of the sandwich board for best results.

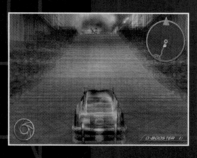

Move toward the stairway at the end of the courtyard and deploy the Q-Booster just before you hit the steps. If you time this move properly, your Aston Martin speeds up, launches through a railing, and jumps over a river and into an Army depot. Congratulations–part one of this mission is complete!

TIP

Failure is not an option, 007. Take care not to execute the Q-Booster too late, launch too soon, or stop accelerating as you hit the stairway. The rule for a successful river leap is to launch as you hit the steps, and keep the accelerator firmly down.

Continue straight ahead into a larger park area, and keep straight to leap to the rooftops ahead. This earns you extra Bond Moves points. Continue along the route, making a second jump down into an alleyway.

Once out of the alleyway, a helicopter attempts to drop grenades on you. Ignore the helicopter–its aim is a little skewed–and instead drive straight through the grassy area. R chimes in, informing you of a present he's left you.

Streets of Bucharest II–Night

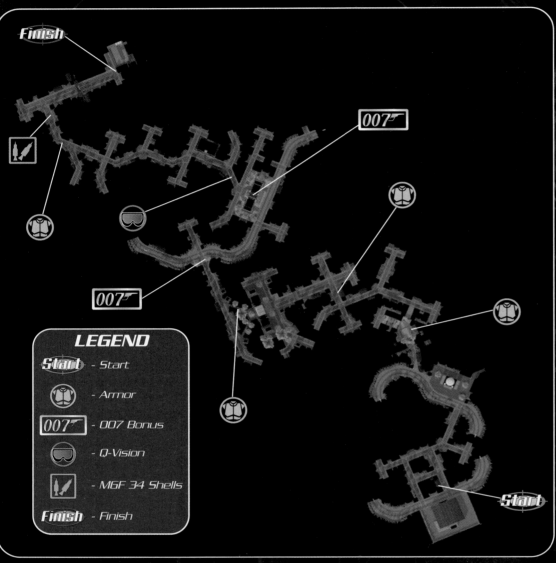

As you trundle down the street attempting to aim proficiently with the Chain Gun (save the cannon for later), two sedans with Rocket-Launcher henchmen appear. Strafe until the left sedan explodes, and then pepper the right one. Tag both before the tank turns right, or these sedans follow up with more shots.

As the tank slowly moves around the corner, swivel the turret to face the rear. A limo screeches out of a side street to the left. As soon as you spot it, take out its engine or wheels with the Chain Gun, or aim at the Machine Gun-wielding enemy first.

Now turn back to face the front, and aim at an incoming car in the distance. This enemy is moving out of a nearby side street. With careful aiming, you can destroy it before it reaches you. Destroy it quickly–this sedan fires Rockets.

Into an armory with an Aston Martin, and out with an MGF-34 Combat Tank! The remainder of this mission has you at the turret of this heavily armored machine aiming at almost everything that moves. Don't worry about the driving, but concentrate on hitting every enemy you can.

LEGEND

Start - Start

- Armor

007 - 007 Bonus

- Q-Vision

- MGF 34 Shells

Finish - Finish

Turn down an alley to the right. Spot a guard on the other side of the bridge and two Rocket Launcher henchmen at the far side of a courtyard. Immediately aim at the guard, then take out the two enemies (and the waiting van) by hitting the oil barrels on the left side of the courtyard. Pick up an Armor in this area.

Now switch to the Tank Cannon. As you enter the archway on the right, you come to a halt, and two sedans pull out in front of you. Take careful aim and demolish them both.

Now switch back to the Chain Gun. Swing the turret around to face the front, and the hovering helicopter ahead. Take out the gunner and continue rapidly firing Chain Gun rounds until the helicopter explodes. If you continuously miss, the chopper flies overhead. Swing the turret round, aim up, and take care of this menace with gusto.

Spin the turret to face forward as the tank trundles on, and wait for a sedan to pull up in front of you. This is an ideal opportunity to tear it apart with the Chain Gun or Tank Cannon. After a right turn, you snag an Armor.

After another street block, you see a large bridge ahead, brimming with enemies. A helicopter fires Rockets at you, a van waits atop the bridge, and a limo stops underneath it. All are readying ordnance to launch at you!

The helicopter fires off a salvo that misses you. When the cutscene ends, fire your Chain Gun or Tank Cannon at the helicopter until it explodes. The remaining troops do little damage, so tag the helicopter first.

Twisted helicopter remains fall from the sky and hit the bridge, blowing it up and eliminating all nearby enemies.

Continue down the road, over some sandwich boards, and through a pillared museum entrance. As you spot the third Armor of this zone, make sure both of your guns are pointing forward. Take advantage of this lull in the action to adjust your weapons' viewpoints.

When two vans pull out in front of you select either weapon to pulverize them as they swerve. Cannon shots are particularly amusing to launch, as they buffet the vans with tremendous force. An easier method is also to shoot the oil tanker between the two vans; the ensuing explosion will rid you of both vans, with hardly a scratch to you!

As you approach the hotel, two helicopters hover into view. Use your cannon or Chain Gun to dispatch them quickly, then continue to face forward as the tank rams the hotel lobby.

It is imperative that you face forward as you head through the hotel lobby. As you emerge from the hotel, you automatically don a pair of Q-Vision goggles with enough power to last 80 seconds. The goggles allow you to spot henchmen from a distance.

Next, a helicopter appears from the left and fires Rockets at you, speeding up to pass overhead before turning and firing at you from behind. Fire at it, pivot, and strike it down from behind. You'll absorb at least one Rocket hit.

As you break through the hotel, train your Chain Gun on the henchman on the first rooftop, slightly to your left. Then target all firepower on the limousine weaving in front of the tank.

Now quickly face the turret forward and anticipate a shot from a henchman on a rooftop to your left as you rumble around the corner. Anticipating the henchman's attack frees up time for targeting distant enemies. Then strike a second henchman who appears from around a corner.

Directly in front of you is another henchman on a building at the other end of the street. Strafe him until he falls. Keep your turret forward as you turn left.

Around another corner, spot and tag a henchman standing on a rooftop directly in front of the tank. Remove him from play, switch to the Tank Cannon, and keep it aimed forward.

Spot the two henchmen with Rocket Launchers on opposite sides of the street, and stop them from connecting with their ordnance. Strafe these two as quickly as possible.

Almost immediately, a van races past you from the left. Hit it once with the cannon as it comes into target range, and a second time as it stops abruptly. This explodes the van before a henchman with a Rocket Launcher appears.

You're almost to the final stretch, so keep your cool and keep that turret facing forward! As you round the corner, swing the Chain Gun slightly left to down the two henchmen on the street.

Ahead is a crate of cannon shells, and their necessity is soon apparent—as you round the corner, you see two enemy tanks under a two-arched bridge, ready to pulverize you with cannon shells.

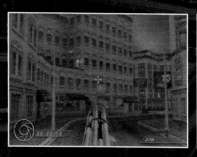

Now move your Chain Gun up to aim at the rooftop ahead on the left. There's another enemy up there. Aim slightly right as you round another corner, and take out two more foes. Take care now—this sortie is almost over!

This is the final fight of this mission, and you must be cunning to survive. The tanks are indestructible—your weapons don't damage the tanks enough to cripple them.

Steady that gun and train it on the barrels to the left of the sedan straight ahead on the left side of the street, near two more henchmen. The explosion takes care of the sedan and the two men with one shot.

Furthermore, these tanks begin to fire at your almost immediately, quickly whittling down your Armor and destroying you in moments. You must hatch a plan, and fast!

Zoom in ahead with the Chain Gun, and tag the guard on the rooftop. Prepare to fire at the limousine pulling up from a road on the left. With good aim and timing, you can explode the limo before it stops.

By now, your Q-Vision goggles should be almost out of battery power. Zoom in with your gun and take out the henchman on the left side of the street. This leaves one airborne unit. Use the Chain Gun to destroy the helicopter, and switch to the Tank Cannon as soon as the helicopter has exploded. Pick up the final Armor.

Fortunately, the freight train moving over the bridge above the tanks is the answer. After every four cargo trucks, an oil carriage passes over the bridge. Piercing this tanker with a cannon shell spells the end of the bridge and the tanks. Ready your aim, ignore the tank fire, and time your shells to hit the carriage. This means firing just after the first cargo truck passes. With a little tweaking of the aim, you hit a tanker and take down the enemies. Bond achieves his final mission objective and delivers the Data Chip to R.

Fire & Water

MI6 Briefing

007, our analysis of the Data Chip reveals that the location of Poseidon is an oil-drilling platform in the South China Sea. While it seems an unlikely location for a cloning lab, you must investigate the site immediately.

Sources in Hong Kong inform us that Bloch has recently boarded a helicopter bound for the oil rig. If you find Bloch, chase him down. We must do whatever we can to hinder Malprave's actions.

R has equipped you with a special means of transport: the Q-Jet. This remarkable device provides a short burst of vertical thrust that propels you into the air. You can use it to leap up to platforms or overcome obstacles.

Ingeniously, the Q-Jet can be fueled by any source of compressed gas you might find in the field. Keep an eye out for sources that might power the device.

Classified Information-Mission Overview

A vertical trek up a giant oil rig is only the beginning of the challenges in this mission–there's much to explore and avoid, and a general feeling of being over-whelmed by enemy forces. Persevere however, and you'll learn how to climb to the summit of this oil rig, chasing Bloch at every opportunity.

Your Q-Jet is an excellent piece of equipment, allowing you to leap around 30 feet in height and length. But if you don't feel like using this device, you can complete the level without it. Crucial to completing this level is the ability to use the scenery to your advantage (by hiding or blowing it up) when facing new enemies, and a fast pair of legs. Keep moving, prime your Q-Laser, and locate Bloch as fast as possible.

Oil Rig-Night

   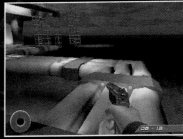

As the dark clouds gather overhead, 007 drops down onto an auxiliary platform in the South China Sea, and immediately silences his P2K. There's no energy for your jetpack, so don't try it out. Instead, gaze up at the tower you're about to infiltrate.

Start by moving around the back of the crates, and check the Armor in one corner. You can pick it up later into your mission if needed, but it's a long backtrack. Move directly off the platform and onto the pipe walkway.

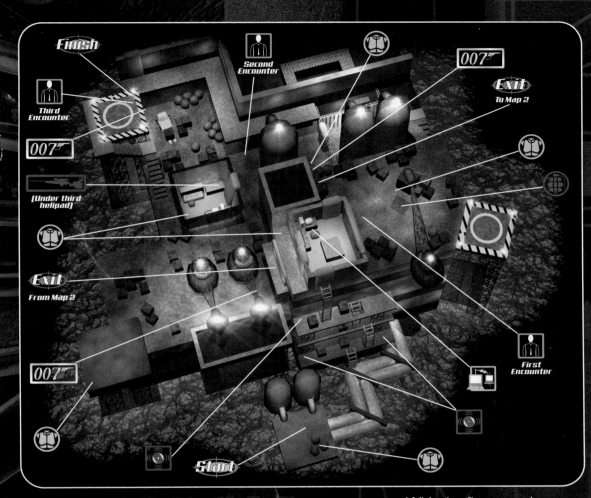

LEGEND

 - Start

 - Alarm Button

 - Nigel Bloch

 - Frag Grenades

 - Q-Remote Terminal

 - Armor

 - Sniper Rifle

 - 007 Bonus

- Exit

- Finish

With the first guard downed, pick up his Calypso Machine Gun, and reload your P2K–use it for as long as you can to conserve ammunition for the weapons you pick up. Now ascend the second set of steps and plug the guard on patrol with three shots.

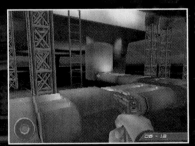

As the structure creaks, look at the three platforms linked by ladders. Locate the first metal ladder, and ascend to the top of the first platform. On the platform, turn right and charge the first guard, plugging him with P2K fire.

TIP

Look up at the first platform before you ascend the ladder to gauge whether the enemy is walking to your left or right as you emerge. This makes takedowns quicker and provides you with the locations of the guards if you ascend the structure immediately.

Now comes the tricky part–two guards patrol the third platform, and if you've made noise of any kind (used an unsilenced pistol, or made the second guard yell "Intruder!"), they'll be ready at the top of the third ladder. Hopefully, you'll be able to surprise at least one by being stealthy, and tagging one as he patrols near the hole in platform three's entrance.

Now climb up the ladder, whether the two guards know your location or not, and clamber to the top, even if you're being hit by bullets. Immediately turn left, and dispatch one or both guards. One is hiding behind the crate to the left of the ladder while the other is likely to be either standing next to him, or has raised the alarm.

BEING BOND

Did that guard press the alarm? Then prepare for more frantic combat. Start by turning off the alarm button. Next, switch to the Calypso.

The remaining guards in this area are alert, and another guard appears on the helipad high up on your right side as you climb. This henchman's intentions are clear—he's trying to lob Grenades your way. Eliminate him.

Also notice a helicopter gunship hovering over the helipad—this doesn't bode well. The gunship is carrying a number of guards to deposit at the base's second helipad. If the alarm has sounded, the gunship lands on the first pad.

Striking the helicopter with Calypso gunfire damages it severely—smoke billows from its tail. Keep plugging at it, and it eventually explodes. This means you won't have to deal with it when you reach the helipad.

NOTE

Swan diving off the side of an oil rig, 007? Are you barking mad? From the third platform, climb on a crate and leap off the edge. If you hit the water, you drown—that Q-Jet you're wearing is weighty, but leaping off the oil rig into the water at any stage ends your mission. If you land on the piped walkway, however, you incur some damage, but live to return to the rig's platforms.

Reload your weapon, switch to the Calypso if you haven't already, and inspect the left portion of the third platform. Here you spot two cranes holding boxes, and behind the cranes are a large courtyard and another helipad. This is where you're headed. Now climb the final ladder.

At the top of the ladder is a control room bathed in green light. Ahead, a technician fiddles with a computer. Quickly give him some gunfire, and then climb into the room. Wait—there's Bloch! He's willing to give you a tour of this facility, along with a frantic gun battle. When he finishes speaking, fire or move at him until he runs away.

You must apprehend Bloch. But first, inspect the immediate area. Once Bloch flees, you see a crate-filled courtyard adjacent to the control room and the helipad. If you've taken out the helicopter, the place is empty, save for a couple stray guards. If not, the helicopter lands. The silence is ominous.

TIP

If there's a helicopter on the helipad, attack it before you exit the control room, while it's stationary. Then you won't have to dodge its bullets once the locked door is opened.

Move to the computer terminal, picking up the Pistol of the guard you just tagged. Produce your Q-Remote, and activate it. It learns the crane release program, allowing you to point your Q-Remote at any crane holding a crate, and lowering or dropping that crate. This could be useful later in this sortie.

If you didn't destroy the helicopter, it takes off, litters the control room with bullets, and then moves to the second helipad. If you already destroyed the helicopter, only the four guards are left. They peek out from crates, trying to locate and fire at you.

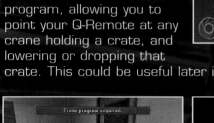

You could activate the crane in the courtyard, but for now turn around, and open the door that isn't locked (to the left of the computer). The door leads to a narrow platform that gives you an excellent vantage point. Study this area; you may wish to use the Q-Remote here later.

Exit the control room via the door you just unlocked, and wade into the fray, taking out all four guards as quickly as possible. If a guard is hiding or standing near a barrel, take the barrel out. Do not stop running, stepping behind crates as cover, and firing until you've downed all of the guards. Running at guards and firing also works.

Now move back into the control room and head for the locked door armed only with your Q-Laser. Remove the lock, and then switch back to a fully-loaded Calypso Machine Gun—four enemies appear behind the crates in the courtyard,

each one training their weapons at you. The four guards only appear after you cut the door lock.

BEING BOND

Point your Q-Remote at the crane winch. The Q-Remote releases the crate, and it smashes onto the ground, exploding the two barrels nearby. This is an excellent choice if you want to take out any guards in this area.

Even if you don't drop the crate during combat, once the area is secure, step away from the immediate area and drop the crate anyway—it contains two Frag Grenades.

NOTE

If you raised the alarm earlier but didn't shoot the Grenadier, he's still on the helipad, chucking Grenades. Trouble is, during combat the four other guards can walk onto these Grenades, making combat all the more frantic.

Now head down the steps after reloading your Calypso—the situation is likely to take a turn for the frenzied. As you reach the bottom of the steps, produce your Q-Laser and hug the right-side mesh fence.

Bloch is behind the fence, taunting you while one of his compadres attempts to strafe you with gunfire from a platform above and to the right. Ignore the mocking and gunfire, and laser through the lock. Bloch runs for cover as soon as you break through.

BEING BOND

To complete your oil rig excursion with minimal wounds, try this method of infiltration. Start by taking out the guard standing on top of the platform next to where you lasered the mesh door lock.

Don't venture forward. Instead, turn immediately right, laser the lock of the maintenance duct, and crawl inside. Turn right, then right again. Produce your Q-Laser, take off the lock, and emerge in the enclosed area on the other side of the mesh door you just opened. Move around the open duct hatch.

Now climb up the ladder onto the platform you saw the guard on before. If you didn't tag him, do so now and clamber up and onto the platform. Move along the platform to the corner.

Bloch! He's managed to run to the second helipad, and is torturing you with a combination of witty banter and heavy ordnance. You've been spotted, and the best plan is to run along the platform, taking out the first guard before he has time to inflict much damage on you.

As the bullets whiz around you, focus on the sniper on the platform to your left. Run in as fast as you can, drowning him in Calypso bullets. By now, Bloch has made his escape, but the small bridge between the helipad and the door to the pump room has been raised. Enter the pump room door. This way is quick, but you'll miss many valuable pickups and you won't confront so many enemy guards.

This area next to the pump room door is an interesting spot from which to fight the main courtyard's many foes—you have the cover of the raised bridge, and a good vantage point to fire at the incoming guards.

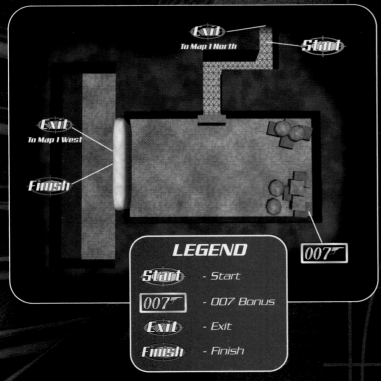

LEGEND

Start	- Start
007	- 007 Bonus
Exit	- Exit
Finish	- Finish

Now turn to the shutter door to your right. Open it by pressing the button to the left of the door. You're now adjacent to cranes two and three—you saw them from the small balcony next to the control room.

Produce your Q-Remote, and point it at the top of the pulley of crane two. This lowers the crate, allowing you to run and drop onto it.

Do not *jump* from the balcony to the crate, or you may overshoot and fall. So once you're on a crate, only look around—don't move at all—this jumping can be disorienting. If you fall, turn around and climb up the ladder.

Once you're on crane two's crate, lower crane three's crate. Then, turn and take out the enemy that may be taking potshots at you from the platform in the distance. This may take some time, but keep plugging away.

Now look up, point the Q-Remote at crane two, and raise the crate to its initial position. Then, look at crate three and drop down to it. Again, jumping results in overshooting, and your demise.

Look up while you're on crate number three, and activate your Q-Remote again. This raises the crate you're standing on. *Now* jump. Face the main courtyard area, and run and leap over the safety rail and into the courtyard.

If dashing across a platform isn't your idea of stealthy infiltration, there are other ways to go. Through the mesh door, instead of turning immediately right, turn left and head directly to another locked grating on the opposite side, near a huge oil container and Armor. Turn and take out the guard on the platform prior to lasering the lock.

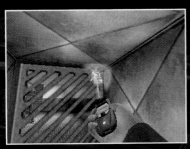 

In the duct (make sure you didn't venture into the main area, or you'll have major headaches sneaking around and enemies attacking you as you enter the duct), ready your Q-Laser and rip through the lock at the other end. Then look left, plant two bullets in the stack of barrels, and subdue the two patrolling guards.

TIP

If Bloch has already spotted you and entered the courtyard before you move over the crates, the gun emplacement is already exposed. This means you have to deal with a number of extra foes, making this jumping extremely difficult. Forget the crate method of entering the courtyard if Bloch has seen you.

When you jump underneath the gun emplacement, a gunship appears at helipad two, lands, and deposits some guards before strafing you with gunfire. Sometimes it finishes with a Rocket attack before flying out of view to the other side of the pump room.

Above you, the gun emplacement opens up, revealing two guards–one armed with Grenades. They stay in position. Whether you enter the courtyard via the crates or by simply running in from the mesh gate, Bloch laughs from atop the second helipad, and commands his henchmen to attack.

The four soldiers running down from the helipad take refuge behind boxes. They're prepared to wait you out, so you must wait until they pop up, then aim slightly above them and fire until you drop them all. Reinforcements may take cover behind the boxes, and to the right of the central control room.

Aim at the barrels in the main courtyard (either on foot or from behind the nest). The stack of barrels under the platform destroy pieces of the platform, but even if both areas of it blow up, you can jump the gaps.

If you entered via the crates and moved directly to the Machine Gun nest, some of the guards that ran down the steps of helipad two may be waiting for you underneath. If so, turn as you drop down from the gun emplacement, and quickly take out these guards.

TIP

You may want to stay in this area and take down guards until the area is secure–each guard drops a weapon with ammunition in it, meaning you're not likely to run out of bullets later.

Get to the gun emplacement as soon as you can–climb up the steps and take out the two guards, or tag them from below. Once on top, move to the Machine Gun nest, and activate it.

Find more barrels and a forklift carrying a pressurized canister–always excellent to take out guards hiding nearby. Use these objects to down guards that you can't effectively aim at.

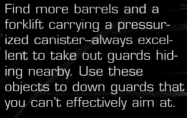

This weapon is perfect for securing the area. Start by aiming at the sniper on the far platform–shoot at the barrels beneath him–the barrels explode, collapsing the platform and taking out the sniper.

Finally, aim at the boxes at the front of helipad two, where Bloch stands. Once you hit him or the crates nearby, he activates the small bridge and escapes to the pump room. Follow him, either via the platform, or up the steps to helipad two, and over the bridge Bloch just used.

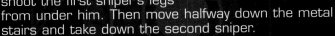

TIP

When the battle is over, move around the courtyard picking up the weapons from the fallen foes. In addition, move to the central tower to bag the Armor, and the Sniper Rifle in the locked case–use the Q-Laser to get in. There's another suit of Armor under helipad three. Watch out for reinforcements!

Oil Rig–Pump Room

You finally made it! But the fun's just beginning. Step out from behind the crates, and take out the two guards hiding behind more stacks of crates. A third guard may either be behind the crates in the corner or running up the steps. Take him out before optionally refilling your Q-Jet at the compressed-gas station on the left wall and taking the Armor.

As you descend the stairs, you see the red laser of a Sniper Rifle. There are two snipers in the central area of the pump room, both on the second level. These must be tackled first. With the Sniper Rifle, stand on the balcony, duck down, and shoot the first sniper's legs from under him. Then move halfway down the metal stairs and take down the second sniper.

TIP

From halfway down the metal steps, you can take out the two snipers and the two guards on the opposite balconies.

NOTE

If you forgot your Sniper Rifle, head to the bottom of the stairs. Switch to your Windsor's Grenades, and aim up or pepper the snipers with Machine Gun fire. There are more guards waiting, and a fierce firefight to deal with.

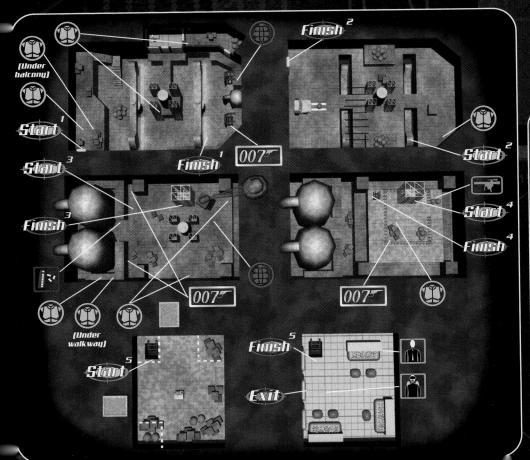

LEGEND

Start	- Start
	- Nigel Bloch
	- Defender Ammunition
	- Rig Diver
	- Frag Grenades
	- Armor
	- Defender
	- MRL-22 Rocket Launcher
007	- 007 Bonus
Exit	- Exit
Finish	- Finish

At the bottom of the steps, use one more Sniper Rifle bullet to take out the guard walking along a curved balcony at the far end of the pump room, on the right. He may already have spotted you.

Through the lattice-shaped scaffolding, spot another guard—this one waiting tentatively with Grenades. He's on the curved balcony to the left of the one you just secured. From the bottom of the steps, face the back of the room and find the guard. Then fire. This saves you headaches as you continue.

At the bottom of the stairs, make a sharp right, head around the huge white metal pipes and around the two sets of barrels to find Armor. If you don't need Armor now, remember its position for later.

There are two more guards to take out in the immediate vicinity, both on the ground floor. They may have heard the sniper fire at you, so watch your step and switch to automatic weapons. Tag each guard as you encounter them.

The compressed-gas canister in the middle of the pump room makes an excellent weapon. As one of the final foes closes in, shoot the valve at either side of the canister to spray intoxicating gas at your victim. Good takedown, 007–but don't get hit yourself.

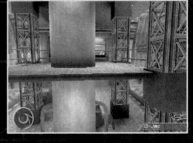

Next, fill your Q-Jet, and take off–land on the central balcony where the snipers were. Stay behind the central pillar for cover, and tackle both Guards as they storm your position. The Calypso or the Windsor is your weapon of choice. If you're overrun, simply drop down, refill your Q-Jet, and leap up to finish the job. Before combat, grab both Sniper Rifles.

A second alternative is to pass the Q-Jet refueling station, and head directly for the balcony where you took down the guard with the Grenades. Climb up the ladder, take the Grenades, and then stop. Two Guards hide in the storage area just ahead. Throw a Grenade through the door to attract them, and then switch to a Machine Gun. As each guard appears, stand your ground and fire until both are defeated.

When the room is clear, move directly into the pump control room and press the pump activation switch. The two gigantic pumps start to move up and down, and Bond spots the only way out–up through the gap to the level directly above the pump room. Stand on the pumps and leap up.

Drop to ground level and take out the two Guards there. Running at them with a Machine Gun blazing works well, but keep moving! Take out these two Berserkers before you turn your attention to the Grenadier on the balcony you stepped onto when you first entered the pump room.

After optionally refueling at the central stations, climb a ladder up the curved balcony you've not yet ascended, and move to the second giant pump arm. Step onto the piston head as it descends to its lowest point. Mistime, and you fall. Stand on the head of the pump and ascend to the next floor, leaping or Q-Jetting out onto solid ground.

CAUTION

Do be careful, 007–you can't step over the hashed areas that the pumps move in and out of, so don't accidentally fall into them, especially when landing on the pump head.

Now on the third floor of the pump room, attack and dispose of the four guards in this area. Start by hitting the canister carried by the forklift ahead of you. That takes care of one guard. Then run around the central pillar, disposing of the rest. Rapid fire and movement are vital here. There's a much needed armor in a dark corner near where you first entered this space.

NOTE

Take out as many of Malprave's barrels as possible. Just keep away from the detonation.

Upon entering the foot of the oil rig tower, notice two huge oil containers in front of you. Above are two balconies, each housing a guard. The one on the left has a Sniper Rifle. Run forward and to the right, and climb ladder to the right-hand container before you're shot.

BEING BOND

With Sniper Rifle in hand, use the cover of the door to take out the sniper on the left balcony, and then finish his friend. This can be tricky, because the sniper spots you immediately. Be patient and aim well.

At the top of the container, move onto the balcony, take the guard down if you haven't already, and then finish his chum. Now comes the fun part–use either your Q-Jet or Q-Claw to leap the gap between the balconies and retrieve the Sniper Rifle and Armor. Then Q-Claw back to the first balcony.

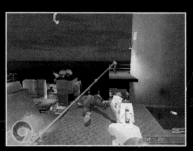

If you fall off the balcony and want to quickly return, simply Q-Claw the meshed areas on the container. Note that under the huge containers there is well hidden Defender ammo and some Armor.

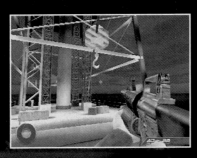

After disposing of the two guards, head for the hook, jump straight up, grab it, and slide along the wire down to the oil rig tower. Grab the hook to activate it. When you land, take cover!

A firefight commences, with four armed guards rushing you, diving for cover behind boxes, and another guard with Grenades in the far left corner of the platform. Start by taking out the guard closest to you.

Then take out the two guards milling around to the right of the central pole, and listen for the sounds of an elevator–two more guards are coming to investigate. Take them out before heading for the final guard with the Grenades. If you get in trouble there is plenty of Armor on this platform–three sets if you are playing at operative level.

If you're quick and activate your Q-Remote, you can point it at crane four and drop the crate on the Grenadier. However, shooting him is easier and less dangerous. When the dropped crate explodes, take the Grenades and move quickly to the elevator the two guards came down on. Activate it.

At the top of the elevator, you reach a covered room with a number of barrels and crates. A voice from a loudspeaker tells you to stop–another helicopter gunship! It appears behind you, to your right after you turn.

Helicopter Gunship Battle

The gunship strafes the building you're in, so move away from any exploding barrels, and aim with your Windsor or Calypso, continuously pumping bullets into the helicopter until it blows up.

You can target the helicopter pilot, and use a Sniper-Rifle to deal with him. This makes combat slightly quicker (the helicopter is downed with one shot!), but it isn't easy. Instead, locate the two barrels to the left of the exit doorway, blow them up, and secure the Rocket Launcher.

Use the Rocket Launcher against the gunship. Watch the guard rails when you aim up at it, or you'll detonate a Rocket at point-blank range.

With the gunship gone, pick up the Armor in this room and run out of the entrance, around the perimeter of the platform, and up the metal ladder to the last area before the top of the rig.

As you climb to the top of the ladder, prepare for the welcoming committee—two snipers and a guard throwing Grenades. As you finish your ladder climb, switch to your Sniper Rifle and plug the guards standing on the concrete slabs suspended by cranes.

There are two ways to ascend to the third platform where the grenadier is standing. The easiest is to simply point your Q-Claw at the mesh area directly above the third platform, and winch yourself up there. Change to a Machinegun, and then drop down and take out the guard with ease—you won't need to worry about leaping the other two platforms.

Or, you can Q-Claw or Q-Jet to the first (or second) of the platforms, refill your Q-Jet if you used it, then turn and fire at the guard from this platform—you can now see him. Dispose of him, then leap or claw to the second platform and then to the highest one. Congratulations—you've almost made it!

BEING BOND

Of course, you can also activate your Q-Remote, point it at the top of the crane that one or both of the snipers are being supported by, and drop the entire slab into the ocean below.

Now there's nothing left to achieve except burning off the lock to the trapdoor overhead. Climb up the ladder, point your Q-Laser, and take out the ladder hatchway.

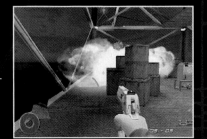

Only that Grenadier remains. He's on the highest corrugated platform that you can see the underside of. Keep moving to avoid those Grenades!

At the top, Malprave's henchman appears behind Bond, pushing him off the oil rig! Bond grabs Bloch as he falls, and they plummet into the swimming pool below. Bloch may still be alive, but you've succeeded in this mission. Excellent performance, Mr. Bond!

Forbidden Depths
Driving Level

MI6 Briefing

Your precipitous leap with Bloch has landed you in the transport system of Poseidon's secret underwater base. Bloch attempts to escape to carry out Malprave's cloning conspiracy. You can't allow that.

The transport system is protected by computer-controlled gun turrets and Bloch's heavily armed forces.

The tunnel structure is too deep and the walls too thick for our radio signals to penetrate them, so you'll be out of contact with us for this one. Good luck.

OBJECTIVE

1. Eliminate Nigel Bloch

Classified Information—Mission Overview

Make a mad dash through the cavernous escape route out of the underwater facility. Don't worry about controlling the tram you're standing in—it automatically drives you to a final battle with Nigel Bloch, the head henchman for Malprave's evil empire.

As the tram hums into life and you start to move down the access tunnel, don't bother cycling through your weapons inventory—you won't find anything except a KA-57 with more than enough ammunition to deal with the enemies to come. Quickly turn 180 degrees, and learn the location of those enemies and gun placements.

Underwater Base Escape Route—Day

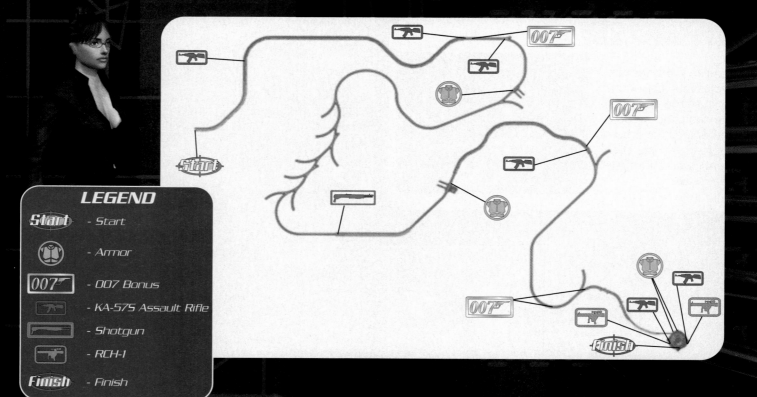

LEGEND

Start - Start

- Armor

007 - 007 Bonus

- KA-57S Assault Rifle

- Shotgun

- RCH-1

Finish - Finish

Take to the tramway at breakneck speed. As the tunnel curves, you notice a henchman standing on the left side–drop him to gain another KA-57. Picking this up gives you extra ammunition.

BEING BOND

When utilizing the KA-57 in this environment, move the weapon about and wait for it to auto-aim, then fire when you are moving through the tunnels at speed. It is never a good idea to manually aim, except when destroying barrels.

Now quickly point your weapon at the roof, and target a metal object with the flashing red lights in the gloom in front of you. This is a turret. There are 9 to take out during this mission, and each fires a nasty spray of bullets if you don't destroy it.

At the bottom of the slope is a henchman standing with a Machine Gun on a tram. If you destroy it (by shooting across the tram and then tackling the enemy) before it starts to move, you can pick up more KA-57 ammunition before entering the security checkpoint.

As both trams start to move forward, you pass under a tower with two henchmen inside. When you shoot the left one, he drops more ammunition.

There are two turrets to take out shortly before the security station. When you hit them, a large explosion rocks the checkpoint, smothering the initial portion of it in thick smoke that slowly dissipates.

As the tram slows to a stop, turn left and quickly aim at the guards behind the glass computer terminal. These guards control the door mechanism beside the terminals. Once they are nullified, the door starts to open.

While you're waiting for the door to open, take out as many guards as you can–this stops them from wounding you with return fire. Look for incoming shots to gauge where an enemy is.

Ignore the henchman through the door in front of you. Instead, shoot the red switch. This opens a blast door ahead. Pick up the Armor in this area as you proceed.

TIP

Immediately tag the henchman with the Rocket Launcher after you clear the security checkpoint; the enemies armed with Rockets cause much more damage than their Machine Gun-wielding brethren.

After another hair-raising lurch around corners, your tram enters a huge glass tunnel. Prepare to destroy another turret at the far end of this section.

The tramway ascends another hill. Destroy the turret that targets you on your way up. Prepare for another henchman on foot.

If you don't take out this tram and its enemy passenger, it will veer off to the right when you run into a T-junction. Meanwhile, you will head left.

On the right-hand side of the tramway, a henchman stands with a Shotgun. Deal with him and he'll drop a Shotgun. Save this weapon until you stop at the warehouse area.

As you continue, another henchman waits on the right farther down the passage. Drop him and prepare for another hill climb.

After the left turn, there's another tram with a henchman on it. Fire your KA-57 directly at the enemy so he doesn't have the chance to retaliate. At the next intersection, the enemy tram crashes headlong into a closed blast door as you pass.

Just prior to entering the warehouse area, you pass under another turret—make it explode as you pass, or you'll lose points and receive a hail of bullets in your back.

Bloch! The arch-henchman finally appears, pulling in front of Bond in his own tram. Shoot until Bloch wobbles, allowing you to automatically reload without receiving much enemy fire. Bloch zips left at the next junction, while your tram heads right. You meet up with Bloch a little later.

The tram slows down and enters a warehouse. Large cargo doors open up to the right. Swing your gun around and train your sights on the barrel behind the four henchmen in this area. Tag it, and the ensuing explosion will deal with them. Quickly train your weapon on the enemy with the Rocket Launcher; use your auto-aim to assist you. Then clean up by dispatching any other henchmen in the vicinity.

BEING BOND

Utilize your new weapon in this zone; the henchmen need only one blast to be sent reeling from the power of the Shotgun. Moving targets, on the other hand, are much more difficult to shoot with this weapon.

As you target the four henchmen in the warehouse to your right, one more guard appears on the platform to your left.

After approximately 10 seconds of combat, a henchman carrying a Rocket Launcher opens the door ahead of you and starts firing. Concentrate your fire on this lunatic—you must dispatch him before you can proceed. You also pick up another Armor in this area.

Where the tunnel starts to wind, four turrets are riveted to the ceiling, and a henchman waits between each of them. Rapid gunning and re-aiming upwards is required—don't miss any of those turrets!

After the battle against the turrets is another tower with two henchmen guarding at the end of this section. Aim for the right window to dispatch a guard who drops another KA-57 ammo item—handy for the constant gunfire to come.

When you speed under the tunnel, Bloch and his tram appear ahead of you once more. He is initially at extremely close range; constantly target Bloch. As you ascend another incline, he begins to pull away.

BEING BOND

When fighting Bloch in this area, utilize the automatic aiming feature of your weapon. This makes it easier to hit both Bloch and the mines he lays.

At the top of the next hill, Bloch edges away, leaving six mines in your path. Explode each one with your KA-57 before your tram reaches them, or you'll receive a nasty jolt.

Toward the end of this section, you face one more turret poking out of the ceiling. Again, destroy the turret.

Bloch evades you one more time, heading left at the intersection, and closing the door behind him. This forces you down a maintenance tunnel much narrower than the previous tramways.

You now must contend with three whirring fans, all of which you must destroy. Failure to take out a fan results in horrific injuries–Bond won't survive more than a couple of these dicing attempts.

The control center is now activated. However, turn your attention to three more henchmen who appear through the same maintenance doors as before. Take them down, and grab the Armor and two bundles of Fly-by-Wire Missiles (RCH-1).

A final hazard waits before the last battle: a section of broken pipe emitting a cloud of hot steam. The steam wounds you, but you can avoid it if you target and hit the two red switches on the left side of the duct. You enter a huge central duct area. The final battle with Bloch is about to commence!

Bloch has opened gigantic doors below, and you can see lava beneath! Now the cooling fan has been compromised from above, and the entire chamber is heating up dramatically.

 First, fire at the bad guys who come in. Then carefully aim at this circular arena's maintenance doors, and the central control unit where Bloch spends most of his time.

You now have limited time in which to defeat Nigel Bloch–if you spend too long locating and firing, you'll succumb to the intense rise in temperature. You're already beginning to feel the heat.

At ground level, three henchmen armed with Machine Guns appear from the ground-level maintenance doors. When you down them with your KA-57s, they each drop an item–Armor and two KA-57s to add to your collection.

Now turn your attention to the plank sticking out of the middle of the central structure–Bloch is on it, and firing wildly. Retaliate with your Machine Gun, and continue to target him until he runs back into the structure.

You mission is straightforward–Mr. Bloch is in the control center, so you must destroy the entire middle of this building. Fire at the three generators at the top of the room using the RCH-1 Missiles. Each generator collapses, destroying the catwalks below, and allowing Bond to finally dispose of Malprave's most persistent henchman.

MI6 Briefing

You've discovered the entrance to Poseidon. This is certainly the laboratory devoted to clone research and production. Your mission is to destroy the laboratory by any means necessary.

Unfortunately, you have no explosives with you. You'll have to improvise some means of destroying the lab equipment. Perhaps your Q-Remote can be used to create havoc with the lab's machinery.

With a program recorded, your Q-Remote can be used to transmit code that will inject harmful chemicals to destroy the unique enzymes and proteins that are required for cloning.

Destroying the lab equipment alerts the base personnel. After you achieve your mission objectives, find a means of escape.

OBJECTIVES

1. Infiltrate clone labs
2. Raise lab equipment temperature
3. Increase lab system pressure
4. Disrupt chemical balance in lab system
5. Board submarine to escape

Classified Information–Mission Overview

Good work on the infiltration, 007—now comes the tricky part—sabotaging Malprave's cloning facilities without being spotted and taken out by her cronies, including Regulation Guards and the more fearsome Berserker Guards she uses. Start by executing a stealthy path into the laboratory, and then swap your P2K for a more destructive and rapid-fire weapon.

Unfortunately, your enemies are also armed with these types of weapons, and they don't hesitate to pepper you with shots, severely cutting down your Armor within seconds. Respond by attacking from cover, taking out barrels, and avoiding firefights. Take each challenge one step at a time, securing a room before completing the objectives, and you'll be in the submarine before you can say "tea and crumpets."

South China Sea–Poseidon Entrance Chamber

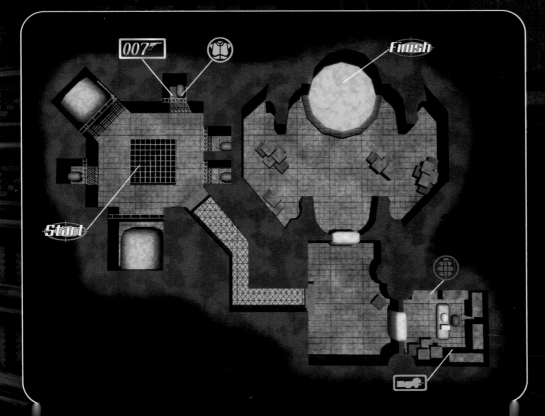

LEGEND

Start	- Start
	- Frag Grenades
	- Armor
	- PS-100 Machinegun
007	- 007 Bonus
Finish	- Finish

Pay attention to the guard behind the computer terminal. Dispatch him quickly before he fires his Machine Gun.

Dropping into a maintenance duct, inspect either of the two locked gratings in front of you. Produce your Q-Laser, and cut the lock off the larger grating. It houses Armor—remember this. Now cut into the narrower duct and crawl into it.

BEING BOND

Confuse your enemy by unlocking the door and crouching behind the crate as it opens. The guard doesn't spot you, and if you crawl forward to the computer monitor then pop up and fire, you can take him by surprise.

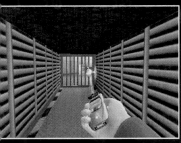

As you advance along this narrow but short duct, produce your P2K, silence it, then switch back to your Q-Laser for the locked grating ahead. A guard patrols in the room on the other side of the grating. When the grating falls away, aim at the guard with your P2K and take him down with a single shot.

NOTE

This area offers more than an opportunity to shoot small vials, 007. There's a PS100 Machine Gun to take, plus ammunition and Grenades. Smash as much lab equipment as you want.

BEING BOND

If you miss your intended target, either shuffle into the room and run around the enemy, or retreat into the duct. The problem is the fast-firing weapon your foe uses—you'll be hit if you fail to tag the guard with your initial one or two shots.

Now comes the other door. This one opens with a simple button-push, and on the other side are two heavily armed guards behind boxes. If you open the door and stand to one side, you can quickly aim at the left guard's head before he attacks.

Once the guard falls, bring out your Q-Decryptor and do a number on the door lock next to the crate. The door swings open, allowing you access to a storeroom.

With the first guard reeling, enter the room, swing around and plug the second guard to the right. Keep firing with the PS100 until the guard falls, and then scout the room for dropped weapons—including more Grenades. Once the room is secure, head to the blue elevator and activate it.

OTE

you were injured in that last battle, return to the
ntrance chamber and secure the Armor in the
econd grated alcove.

ou appear in a viewing chamber with a glass case that
ouses a very large shark. Unfortunately, two capsules
ppear from either side of the case, each housing a
erserker Soldier. As soon as you enter this room, run
r either of the two doors behind you, one on the left
all, the other on the right wall.

BEING BOND

t is possible to take out
oth Berserkers without
suffering too much harm.
First, move to the back of
the room, behind one
capsule.

Then, as the Berserker
appears, rattle off fire. By
the time he turns around,
you should have hit him
enough for him to fall.
Now turn your attention
to the other Berserker.

He's probably shot
through the glass of the
shark case, but fire rapidly at him from the other
side of the case, and he
won't charge straight at
you with guns blazing—his
most damaging attack.

Now at the laboratory
entrance, immediately run in
and take out the guard
standing in the middle of the
room, and then sidestep to
one of the two arched
doorways. Two haz-mat
suited guards are also ready
to attack.

Quick bursts of PS100
fire work well—take the left
haz-mat guard down
first—there's Armor in his lab
area—and then immediately
target the other. When combat is over, head back into the
central corridor and open the
door ahead.

South China
Sea-Poseidon
Clone Laboratory

LEGEND

 Start - Start

 - Armor

 ACCESS - Verification Code Card

 - Q-Remote Terminal

 - Laser Activation Button

 - Frag Grenades

007 - 007 Bonus

Finish - Finish

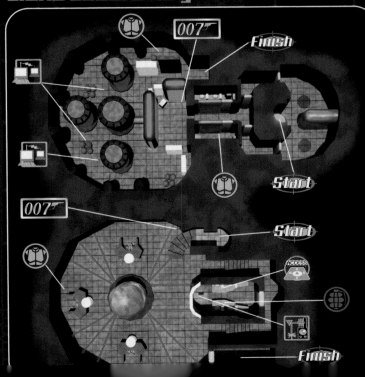

Additionally, one guard hides behind boxes in the corner of the room near the computer terminals. Take them all down.

This room houses three giant vats of proteins essential for the growth of Malprave's army. Your job is to halt the production of these inhuman beings. Start by running left, around computer terminals, and between the first two vats, tagging the guard walking away from you.

Now run forward with Machine Gun blazing, and remove the second guard. If you run in without stopping, you can dispatch these two guards without suffering any damage.

With the guards out of the picture, activate your Q-Remote, and move to the mini-terminal near each vat. These consoles have information on the clone protein terminals in another part of the base, and you must download this information. Do this once for each vat.

Now turn right and head straight for the guard wandering about around the third vat. Run at him, and finish your strike standing near the window next to the third vat. This gives you time to turn around and take out the fourth guard, who's moving between the third vat and the central pipes.

Now to exit. As you run toward the blue elevator door between the third vat and the central pipes, a Berserker Guard charges out of the doorway. Be ready for this attack, and immediately strike back with the PS100, or the UGW you've just acquired.

By now, three more guards have been called in for back-up. Backtrack to the first two vats, and watch for guards running at you in the area where you took down the first two guards.

Prior to leaving, check your Armor–if you need a boost, check behind the second vat for a suit of Armor and behind the three barrels to the left of the exit door for another suit of Armor. Aim at a barrel to explode it (don't stand too close!), and then collect the second Armor before exiting and taking the elevator down.

As the elevator doors open, you enter a large cloning facility with four armed guards, three haz-mat suited guards each watching their own cloning terminal, and a huge central cylinder filled with DNA samples. Also of note are the two rather large Sentry Guns bolted onto the ceiling.

Start by checking the Sentry Guns. Then look to your left. See the guard patrolling that cylindrical area? Wait for him to walk out of view.

Now sprint down the steps, turn left, and head through the doorway, up the narrow steps, around to the right, and then sharply right again, into the main computer terminal security room. Immediately take down this guard.

If you're not swift enough or the guard in the security room sees you run down the stairs, he'll attempt to activate the security system—the console button at the cylindrical end of the room.

TIP

No matter what happens, do *not* activate the security system button unless the guards are patrolling at the far end of the room. Either you can get them caught up in "friendly fire," or they'll skip past the laser beams and ambush you in the Control Room. This makes the next part of the mission extremely difficult!

You tagged the guard in the security terminal? Excellent! Now take the Verification Code Card from the computer bench to the right of the security button, and head back into the main lower laboratory room—there are six guards to take down.

Concentrate on attacking the three black-suited guards first. Keep firing, and stay near the two entrances to the security room in case the guards try to run back there. They can move and attack you from behind, and they usually run around the central vat to attack, so stay in partial cover and keep firing until all three fall.

The remaining three haz-mat suited guards are easy to take down, because they stand their ground at each of the three terminals. Run around behind the guards (time it just after they start to reload) and tag them. Don't forget the extra Armor near the middle terminal!

BEING BOND

That guard pressed the security button, didn't he? If he did, and you're in the enclosed security area, three guards run in and attack. Take them down from inside the security area (after attacking the guard in this zone), and prepare for a spot of laser-leaping.

BEING BOND
CONTINUED

When the guard activates the security alarm, a string of lasers appear on the ground and in the air, criss-crossing the entire chamber. If you or a guard trip a blue wire, the Sentry Guns are activated. They'll gun you down in seconds. If you don't trip the blue wire, you'll need deft jumping to move around the three terminals.

Simply wandering into the main area and firing at guards can start well, but this alerts the guard in the security area, and he activates the laser wires.

With the guards incapacitated, move to the first terminal, and activate your Q-Remote. The temperature of the vats rises to critical levels as the virus spreads. Next, the system pressure reaches unsafe levels. At the final terminal, the chemical imbalance is introduced. Your job is almost complete. Now find that submarine!

Locate the door to the right of the security archways, and use the Q-Decryptor to unlock it. Now be ready with the PS100 or UGW—there's a final surprise—a Berserker guard! Take him down with continuous fire, take his UGW Assault Rifle, and climb those steps!

South China Sea-Submarine Dock

You must now traverse a giant submarine dock, somewhat similar to the one encountered in the Orchid Research Facility, but with one important difference—these guards are highly trained! Don't wade in with guns blazing—take out foes from a distance to avoid becoming overcome.

LEGEND
- **Start** - Start
- - Frag Grenades
- - Armor
- - Bridge-lowering Button
- **007** - 007 Bonus
- **Finish** - Finish

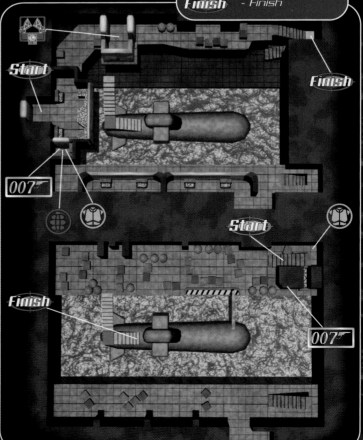

Start your jaunt around this extremely well guarded submarine bay by arming yourself with the UGW Assault Rifle, and taking up a defensive position in the doorway, looking to the right. Use the weapon's scope, and you spot two guards—one throwing Grenades, and the other with a Sniper Rifle. Take aim at their heads and fire until both fall. Then enter the control room.

Hug the left side of the console—don't put yourself in danger by moving into the line of sight of the second sniper—you'll take him out soon enough. Move to the doorway on the left. Stand and fire at the enemy on the walkway.

Now move into the turret area, and take out the sniper. He'll have switched to his Viper, so take both the Sniper Rifle and the Viper when he falls. Then press the console button the sniper was guarding. This lowers the metal bridge, allowing you access to the submarine.

BEING BOND

Tackle the guard on the platform, and then taking the turret sniper from the walkway. Shoot through the glass, take down the sniper, and avoid a vicious attack as you round the doorway into the turret.

NOTE

With the snipers gone, return to the main control tower and enter the right-hand door. Inside the small red-lit store room, there's Armor waiting.

Move quickly along the corridor. Run until you hear shots hitting the walls. Turn and snipe two guards who are firing Machine Guns at you from the opposite side of the loading bay.

Now continue along the corridor, heading down to the bottom of the metal stairs. Only a long narrow loading bay lies between you and the submarine. As you reach the ground, a giant metallic arm swings over. Now snipe the two enemies appearing in the far windows. One fires a Machine Gun, and the other lobs Grenades.

If you run out of Sniper Rifle ammunition, switch to the UGW.

Before you trek down the rest of the lower corridor, turn and retreat behind the steps. Find a suit of Armor and a small hatch that needs to be lasered. At the other end of the duct is a walkway near a number of explosive barrels. Take care when moving from this area back to the main corridor.

As you continue forward, three guards appear from the right-hand walls and take up defensive positions behind crates and barrels in front of you. Take out any explosive barrels, and plug the guard hiding in the crates near the water's edge. Continue forward, and any guards you didn't take down retreat to the end of the walkway.

BEING BOND

There are a number of ways to defeat the heavily armed troops in front of you. Start by hitting explosive barrels—don't stand near them when you move forward and face the next wave of attackers.

Second, try lobbing a couple of Grenades. With appropriate aiming, you can take down a couple of guards at a time—the only problem is adjusting your aim with the few Grenades you have.

Next, try using the Sniper Rifle or UGW to tag distant or running enemies, without engaging in combat and taking damage from Machinegun rounds. Take a shot, and then move to take another so you aren't hit as frequently.

Finally, you can simply advance with a large, fast-firing weapon, and strafe around each enemy to stop them from locking onto you. Take down each one, using the right-hand wall struts as cover.

Don't retreat up to the initial platform or rooms—your enemies follow you up and attack with gusto, and the narrow walkway makes strafing difficult, allowing your foes to hammer home with their weapons.

As you advance, you encounter three more guards, plus any enemies you didn't take down earlier in your corridor jaunt. Use the cover to the right, retreat to more distant cover as necessary, target each enemy until he falls, then switch to attacking the next. Also watch for guards hiding in the alcoves along the right wall.

Bond walks down the ramp and into the submarine, clutching the Verification Code Card that ensures his freedom from this underwater nightmare. He's surprised to discover Zoe Nightshade, who reveals that it was her double that perished. At any rate, good work 007. Now prepare to locate Malprave and put a stop to her hideous machinations once and for all!

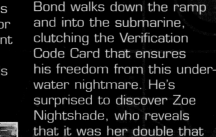

The enemy at the far end of the corridor is dangerous—he throws Grenades in your direction, and because of the reasonably large open space between you and him, he's pretty good at it. When you hear the sound of a Grenade falling, run—either retreat or charge forward and dispatch him before he throws another.

You didn't forget to lower the walkway to the submarine when you entered the turret, did you? If you did, run back to that turret. Now return and run up the walkway. You can shoot at any remaining enemies on the far side of the dock (which you never enter) if you spot any.

Mediterranean Crisis

MI6 Briefing

007, the autopilot steered the submarine to a Royal Navy carrier stationed in the Mediterranean Sea. This ship is the site of a major meeting of the leaders of the world's industrial nations.

Unbeknownst to the public, Malprave's men have taken control of the carrier. The vials of blood you obtained in Hong Kong match the DNA of the eight world leaders. We are certain Malprave has cloned these leaders and intends to substitute them with her clones.

Your first duty is to report to us for an update of the situation. Find the ship's briefing room, where you can establish communications with MI6. We will then provide you with further intelligence data.

```
OBJECTIVES

1. Go to briefing room for MI6 update
2. Disarm warhead
3. Rescue Zoe Nightshade
4. Destroy cloned leaders' helicopter
```

Classified Information–Mission Overview

It's tricky to run through this level unscathed. There are two ways to enter this carrier—as a prisoner (if you didn't retrieve the Verification Code Card in the previous sortie) or via a stealth dinghy. There's no need to tell you which method is preferred.

When you're running through the decks of the *Excalibur*, you encounter guards armed with the most powerful Machine Gun—the PS100. This, coupled with the cramped fighting conditions and your enemies' high levels of training, means you must take down one opponent at a time. Back up into previously explored zones to if the fighting gets too frantic. Then there's the wayward aircraft to worry about, and Q-Clawing up to free Nightshade. All in all, this is the toughest level you've faced.

Entry Point 1: Bond Not Compromised

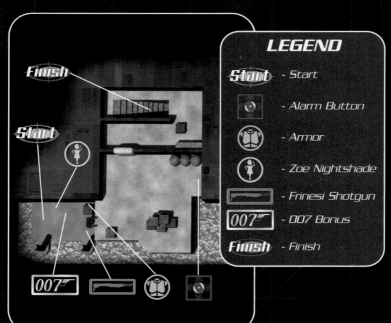

LEGEND

Start	- Start
	- Alarm Button
	- Armor
	- Zoe Nightshade
	- Frinesi Shotgun
007	- 007 Bonus
Finish	- Finish

As the cream of Britain's fighter jets, the Harrier descends onto the aircraft carrier, Bond and Nightshade agree to split up to cover the ship. Your first plan of action is to locate the ship's briefing room for an update from M. Start by edging forward and grabbing the Shotgun from the foot of the small ladder.

The patrolling guard may see you immediately, exclaim something, and run to press the alarm.

React by shooting him with the Pistol or Shotgun, by hitting the barrels, or even by running in and karate-chopping him! Now switch to the Shotgun–there are well-armed soldiers to deal with.

Turn the wheel and open the door just to the left of the barrels. If your guard takedown was noisy (that is, if it wasn't silenced), there's a second guard armed with a PS100 behind the door. Blast him at close range with one well-aimed Shotgun round. Now descend the metal steps into the ship's main corridor.

Forgot the Verification Code Card, did you? Fortunately, your captives failed to find your Q-Laser. Produce it, laser the padlock off when the guard starts his patrol, then run forward and belt him. Run for the table opposite your cell, grab the Shotgun, and blast him.

If you caused a ruckus in the cell or the guard raised the alarm, a couple of guards may have charged down from the briefing room ahead–introduce them to the business end of your Shotgun, and then inspect the area.

Entry Point 2: Bond Compromised

LEGEND

Start	- Start
	- Alarm Button
	- P2k 9mm Ammunition
	- Frag Grenades
	- Armor
	- Zoe Nightshade
	- Frinesi Shotgun
007	- 007 Bonus
Finish	- Finish

Also open the right-hand side entrance, rush in, and overpower the guard patrolling the area–if you don't, he may hear the gunfire from battles to come and attack you from behind. Run into the storeroom when the guard walks left, and explode the gas cylinders behind him.

The noise of the battle alerts three guards, who run in from the briefing room. Start by grabbing the Armor in the storeroom, and then press on into the next chamber prepared to fight. One of the guards is a Berserker, attacking with a Machinegun. Use the narrow confines to your advantage–hem them in, taking down one at a time. If you're accurate and lucky, you can down all three, and then enter the briefing room.

You have a choice–either infiltrate the briefing room via a series of ducts, or a more conventional approach.

BEING BOND

Getting injured? Then conduct a brief sortie through the air ducts of the ship–this is the safest route to the briefing room, and allows you to tag the remaining guards without being hit. (You save ammunition this way too.) Move to the brig, grabbing the Shotgun from the table if you haven't already.

Jog down the passage until you spot the sign that reads "Briefing Room." Follow the arrow left to the briefing room entrance. Immediately left is a storeroom full of explosive barrels. Turn into this room and take out the guard. If you miss him, you'll be surrounded and taken out in seconds.

If you began your mission outside, the cells will be locked, and you must remove the padlock from the cell on the left (as you walk in). Zap it with your Q-Laser (if you started in the Brig, this was your first act), and then move into the second cell, opposite the door. At eye level on one wall is a padlocked grating. Open it with the Q-Laser.

After entering the duct, turn right and crawl parallel to the main corridor. Ignore the grating to your right. The duct turns left, then continues to a grating in the right wall. Q-Laser the padlock to open it. You see a guard in front, standing in the storeroom with the barrels. One well-aimed shot should do it.

When you enter the briefing room, M chimes in, letting you know of Malprave's plans for cloning the world leaders, and about a nuclear warhead that needs disarming. When the conversation ends, exit via the door with the sign reading "Hangar 1". Don't use the stairs just yet; instead, check the underside of them for Armor and two more Grenades. Ascend the steps.

Continue quickly down the duct. A second guard hears the first guard fall, and comes creeping down the corridor to investigate. Meanwhile, turn right, edging down the duct to the next grating, and zapping the lock there. If you're quick, you can tag the next guard from this location. Turn right, hit him before he shouts, and wait here!

Now at the top of the steps, use the UGW's scope to check the hangar ahead. There's a haz-mat suited guard ahead, and three guards patrolling the main hangar area. Eliminate the haz-mat suited enemy, then switch to the Shotgun or a rapid-fire weapon and wait for a second guard to appear. Tag him!

A third guard creeps down from the briefing room. Blow out the canisters behind him to finish him off. Now all that's left of the gang is the Berserker Guard. He runs in, eventually spots you, and lets rip with his rapid-fire weapon. Stand to one side of the duct exit to avoid being peppered, and take him on.

Continue to the end of the duct, zap the padlock on the final grating, and drop into the briefing room. If the Berserker Guard hasn't appeared yet, this is where he'll be. Tag him from cover.

LEGEND

Start - Start

- Frag Grenades

- Armor

- Harrier Program

007 - 007 Bonus

Finish - Finish

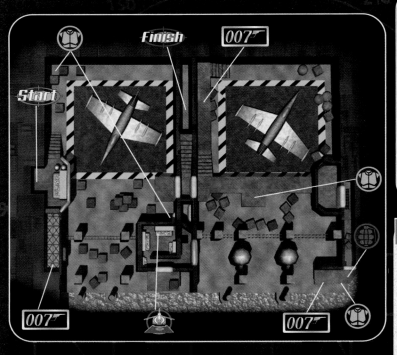

BEING BOND

Alerted too many Berserker Guards? If you get in trouble, retreat up the platform steps, into the control room, and back down the steps to the briefing room. Then turn around and wait for the guards. They stop at the top of the steps. Attack them from the bottom of the steps for increased cover.

When you move down the platform ladder from the control room and run into the main hangar area, a large plane lift descends. There's a Harrier jump-jet on it, along with a Grenadier enemy. Take him out (preferably before you unleash any Berserker Guards).

After taking out the three Berserkers, there are a few options—you can run to where the Berserkers emerged from, and head around the corner, following the signs to the flight deck. However, you'll end up in hangar 2, where more guards aim at you. You don't want that, so turn right instead, and climb the red ladder.

When you venture into the middle area, the door leading to hangar 1 opens to reveal up to three Berserker Guards (the number depends on how stealthy you've been). Switch to the Machine Gun, hide behind the crates, and down the guards.

Of course, there's a much safer, more cunning, and more valuable route through this hangar. Take out the haz-mat suited guard, then turn immediately right, and Q-Laser the padlock off a grating.

Duck down into the duct, and crawl along until you reach another grating on your left.

This leads to a sectioned-off part of the hangar, patrolled by only one guard. Drop onto the hangar ground level, hug the crates for cover, and quickly down him. Now run to the right side of the ship, (this is the side that's toward the ocean). Look up—there's a Q-Claw mesh ahead. You know the plan!

Once you've Q-Clawed up here, take the only door you see before the drop to hangar 2. Move into the doorway. You're now in the control room area (this is the room with the red ladder that a less subtle secret agent would have climbed after clearing the first hangar). Take on the haz-mat suited guard at the controls. If you made any noise nearby or attacked the Berserkers, he'll be ready for you.

Once that is completed, produce your Q-Remote and bring it to the right-hand console. With one button press, it learns the Harrier activation program. Point your

Q-Remote at the back of the plane in front of you, and activate the program. The Harrier's engines roar into life. This could come in handy later....

Now comes the tough part—there are six guards and a sniper prepared for combat in the second hangar. Return to the right side of the ship, drop down to the hangar ground level, and run until you hit another raised area. Look up, Q-Claw again, pick up the Armor, and head for the door at the end of the ship.

The door leads to a short red-lit corridor ending in a second control room. Tackle a haz-mat suited guard—he may be behind the door to the left. From here, you spot a narrow balcony. There's a sniper in the middle, and guards on the floor below. Charge in and tag the sniper before he can strike, then pick up the weapon. There's some sniper fun to be had here—use the sides of the armored walkway for cover, and watch for troops running around the second Harrier, up toward you near the crate stack.

Alternatively, you can drop down the red ladder and charge in, using boxes as cover. Try to tackle the three guards that spot you. This is a tiring battle, with well-equipped guards usually getting the better of you. A way out of this area is around the perimeter of the Harrier jet—but there's a sniper there.

Using either stealth and sniper fire, or dogged melee fighting, clear the area of foes. Check the signs pointing to the flight deck. Take the doorway, turn 180 degrees, and climb the steps. The doorway to the left leads to a balcony overlooking hangar 1.

You can, of course, drop down on the right side, and get ready for the two guards in the area with the steam canisters. Run around those canisters, plugging the valves off so the guards are staggered by the escaping steam. Then, turn your attention to the padlocked gate to the main hangar.

At the top of the steps, Miss Nightshade radios in, letting you know she's secured communications. Turn around and gingerly step forward. There's a Berserker Guard just around that corner!

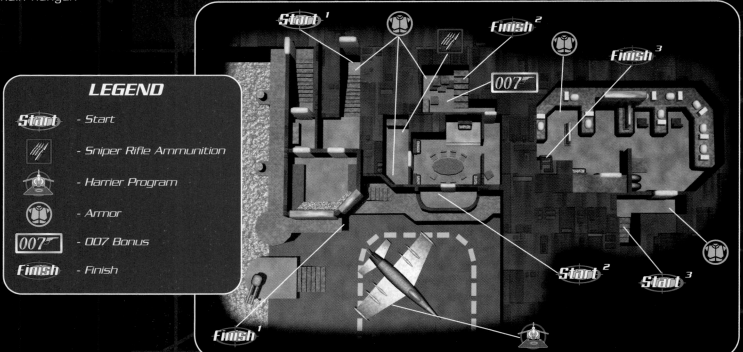

LEGEND

Start - Start

- Sniper Rifle Ammunition

- Harrier Program

- Armor

007 - 007 Bonus

Finish - Finish

Walk forward, poke your head out so he spots you, then dart back and shoot the steam valve in front of you. Pick up the guard's weapon, and move into the flight deck.

You're now in a storeroom leading to the flight deck. Zoe lets you know she's at the conference room, and that there's no sign of clones. Pick up the Armor, and open the door ahead of you. It's time for a little toasting....

Walk up the steps, pausing to dispatch the patrolling guard in the walkway to your right. If you wait, he walks around the control desk and spots you. Take him on with whatever you have (except Grenades), and then run into the small control room. There are three guards on the flight deck—one of them at a Machine Gun nest. Nasty....

BEING BOND

If the guard patrolling the balcony behind this control room charges in, dispatch him. Now it's time to fight fire with fire—Harrier jump-jet fire, to be exact. Break a window, peer down to the three enemies below, and point your Q-Remote at the back of the Harrier.

The jet engines roar into life, eliminating the three guards. This allows you access to the main conference room and upper decks without fighting.

Now turn around, take the left exit up the steps, turn left and left again, and tackle the guard if you haven't already. If you forgot to obtain the Harrier activation program from hangar 1, the going gets tough—you must take out the three guards by lobbing Grenades.

Continue walking past what appears to be a dead end, then turn and look up to your left. There's a Q-Claw mesh above the conference room. Aim quickly, Q-Claw up, and attack the initial guard when you land (he may have already spotted you). If you attack before you reach the top, this area is swarming with enemies.

It's Shotgun time! As the Berserker Guard spots you, either run at him and get two good blasts off, or back up, go to the bottom of the stairs, and then finish him. Now trek back up there!

Use the metal outside walls of the conference room area to shield you from Machine Gun fire from inside. Launch into the room, tackling each guard individually. There are two in the main room, up to two in the left storage alcove, and one to the right, hiding as you exit this chamber. The Shotgun works well here. Don't forget the Armor in the left alcove before you leave!

As you open the door ahead, Zoe tells you that she's just been kidnapped! Time is of the essence, and you must climb a stairwell that has two Grenadiers, a sniper, *and* a Berserker Guard! Run.

On the second floor, turn as soon as you can, and take out the second Grenadier. Run around past the sniper beam, plugging rounds into him, then turn and quickly blast the sniper. Sneaking up doesn't do any good, so charge up and blast at close range with the Shotgun. Now return for the Armor, and grab more Armor at the top of the stairs before continuing.

Quickly run into the lower area to the right of the stairs, grab the Armor from the far corner (or retreat back to get it after combat), and then clamber up the first flight of steps. If a Grenade lands at your feet, either back up or continue on. A moving target is harder to hit. Immediately take out the first Grenade guard.

Prepare for a frantic fire-fight! As you enter, take out the two guards hiding behind consoles, and step in to tackle as many guards as you can before a helicopter gunship arrives, shooting around the entire chamber! Dive back into the initial stairwell, wary of more reinforcements coming up the steps. Then wait for the helicopter to drop out of sight before finishing the final two guards. Let the guards come to you; running into the

BEING BOND

If there's time, and a Sniper Rifle handy (you can take one from the guard on the balcony overlooking the stairwell), quickly plug the gunship pilot with a single Sniper-Rifle round. This makes the combat a lot more subdued, and wins you more points.

On the roof of the control deck, move right, and tag the guard that comes running. Then take out the second guard before he uses the Machine Gun nest ahead of you. If this happens, aim for the barrels behind him, and let the explosion do the rest.

At the end of the fracas, wait for silence, and then move to the ladder at the far end of the room. Careful, two more reinforcements arrive from the stairwell. Look up, procure your Q-Laser, and take out that padlock before climbing up. It's not over yet!

LEGEND

- **Start** - Start
- - Kidnapped Crew Member
- - Armor
- - Missile Program
- - Zoe Nightshade
- **007** - 007 Bonus
- **Exit** - Exit
- **Finish** - Finish

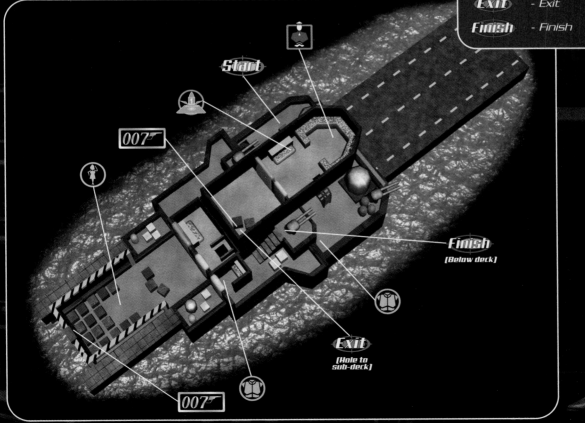

Start
007
Finish [Below deck]
Exit [Hole to sub-deck]
007

TIP

Destroy all the nearby barrels so you aren't hampered by explosions in the firefight.

If you make it to the Machine Gun nest in time, try to hit the gunship before it leaves. A single well-placed Sniper Rifle round to the pilot is much more effective than denting the gunship's Armor with countless rounds of fire. When combat ends, turn and walk to the red ladder behind the Machine Gun nest. Q-Laser the lock and climb up.

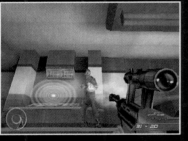

At the top, there's an enemy directly ahead of you. Tag him as you climb out, then swing right and fire on the second guard. Quickly Q-Laser the crew member from her bondage. She opens the doors to the depth charge bay below, where Zoe is being held.

Before you leave, locate the console with the missile launch program on it, and retrieve the information with your Q-Remote. Then, walk through the door and check out Zoe's location. She's dangerously close to highly explosive depth charges!

There are three ways to take care of the two Berserker Guards without having to scrape what's left of Zoe Nightshade off the deck. We'll cover the less safe alternatives first. Move onto the deck, where you can see the enemies, and produce a precise firing weapon (the Sniper Rifle or UGW). Carefully fire at each guard. Hit any barrel, and the entire deck explodes, which is bad.

The second plan is even more foolhardy, and it involves you grabbing the hook, sliding down onto the deck, and facing both guards at close quarters. The potential for exploding depth charges is enormous (both from your foe's weapons and your own), so only choose this method if you're feeling extremely lucky.

BEING BOND

The third plan involves minimum ammo expenditure and no harm to Zoe. Move around the crates on the top deck, and discover a hole. Drop through it onto a lower deck, then move forward, dropping onto the roof of a control room overlooking the depth charges and Zoe.

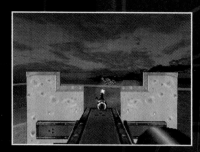

Now find the hatch on the roof, Q-Laser it open, and drop into the control room. From there, it's a simple matter of mashing the large green button on the console in front of you. This activates the mechanical arm, moving it toward you. Zoe grabs the arm, and leaps to cover behind the crates, leaving you to mop up the two Berserkers. Hit one barrel from the doorway, and take out the duo with the depth charges they're standing near.

Run to the deck and activate the Machine Gun nest. Aim the gun at the helicopter gunship on the deck below, and continuously fire at it. Keep firing to explode the helicopter in shards of black metal. The clones are no more!

NOTE

If the helicopter gunship flies overhead and out of range, you must try this mission again.

While Zoe secures a jet fighter for you both to escape in, you must disarm the warhead. Turn around, taking the right-hand doorway to a small room with a long ladder down to the main deck. Descend. At the bottom, M radios in to tell you the cloned leaders are about to flee the ship! Take the Armor at the bottom of the ladder, reload, select your Q-Remote, and open the door.

Suddenly, a Harrier jet launches from the ship. It looks like Malprave has made her final escape. Then, a second Harrier thrusts upward—this one is piloted by Zoe! Turn left, trot down the steps, and get on board. You're following Malprave back to her Alpine hideaway for a final showdown!

As you enter the main deck, turn left, and immediately activate the missile program. This launches a missile, and foils another Malprave plot. Now sidestep right, run down the deck, and immediately gun down the Berserker Guard. There's no time to waste!

Evil Summit

MI6 Briefing

Malprave is holding the world leaders at a base high up in the Swiss Alps. OO7, you must prevent world chaos and global economic meltdown by rescuing the leaders of the world!

The eight leaders are almost certainly being held at gunpoint. You'll have to ensure that none of them come to harm. All eight hostages must survive unscathed.

Once the leaders have been rescued, find Malprave. Be careful when confronting her—no doubt she has more tricks up her sleeve.

OBJECTIVES

1. Infiltrate Alpine Base
2. Rescue eight world leaders
3. Escape silo on elevator
4. Defeat Bloch

Classified Information—Mission Overview

This short final mission pits you against Malprave's troops, and includes a dangerous trek around four giant Missile silos, each containing a world leader that needs to be saved from execution. Then there's a final showdown with Malprave, and a startling confrontation with a henchman you suspected was dead....

For this mission, you need a quick trigger finger and great stealth. These guards are vicious, their weapons (the D-17 Assault Rifle) are deadly, and the way they guard their prisoners doesn't allow for any wrong moves. If you're cunning, you can rescue the world's leaders before their clones can wreak havoc!

Alpine Base—Dusk

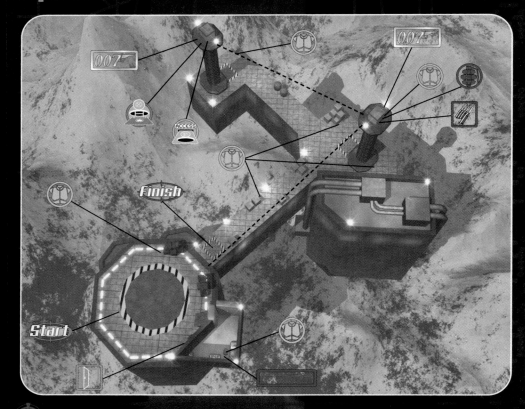

LEGEND

Start	- Start
-----	- Q-Slide Wire
	- Armor
007	- 007 Bonus
	- Frag Grenades
	- Sniper Rifle
	- Sniper Rifle Ammo
	- Doorway
	- Hatchway Program
	- Access Hatch
Finish	- Finish

While Nightshade hovers her Harrier jump-jet on the helipad of Malprave's Alpine Base (the zone you previously visited as Mr. Somerset), survey the loading bay and twin sniper towers in front of you. Four snipers, and you have no powerful weapons...tricky.

Now to take care of those snipers. Find the locked case at the back of the room. Use your Q-Laser to break the lock, and grab the SSR 4000 Sniper Rifle inside. You have two bullets, and there are four guards on the towers. Crouch, turn around, and edge forward.

  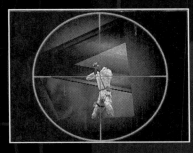 

Before you run down the walkway to the first tower (and receive sniper fire to the chest), look ahead—there's a hatchway on the ground. Download an unlock code from the console in the sniper tower on the left.

Decide which snipers you want to take out—will it be two on one tower, or one on each? Whatever path you chose, don't waste those bullets! We recommend taking out both guards on tower 2, and then storming tower 1—the snipers will switch to handguns as you approach.

The best way to complete this area is to turn slightly right from your starting point until you spot a pair of double doors leading to a security room. Bound up the stairs and open the door, then punch the guard until he falls. Pick up his PS100 and step back from the window, into the rear area of the security building.

Stand up, peer out of the window, and look down at the enclosed walkway leading out of this area. There's a fifth guard here. Not for long. Tag him with your newly acquired PS100, and then look up. A hole in the roof? Maybe that'll come in handy later. Now leave the building.

CAUTION

Don't try any airborne capers like jumping off the towers or the sides of the helipad. Just think of the Q-gadgets you'd destroy!

Back on the helipad, ignore the sealed door to the right of the security area, and head onto the walkway. Run straight past the green crates and to the foot of the right-hand tower. Wait near the elevator for it to descend, then step onto it and ride it to the top. Grab the Armor near the elevator.

At the top, step off the elevator, deal with the two guards if they are still there, grab the two Sniper Rifles (these are vital for a later takedown), then grab the Armor, Sniper Rifle ammo, and Grenades from inside the tower control room. Now turn your attention to the second tower. Descend to the ground, run to tower 2 and ascend it with haste.

BEING BOND

After you receive the hatchway code, at least three guards are always stationed on the helipad (unless you're on the helipad itself, in which case no more appear). These guards hide and crouch before spraying you with gunfire. Be ready!

Guards appear after you ride the elevator down from the first tower, and run to the second one. They appear as you activate the Q-Remote terminal on the second tower.

BEING BOND

You should have obtained the hatchway command in your Q-Remote by reaching the top of tower 2 and programming it in. Guards start streaming out everywhere. Run to the rappelling hook, grab it, and slide to the first tower, then down to the security room. The hole in the roof is for you to drop Grenades down on the enemies, then drop down and move to the helipad before more guards appear.

Alternatively, you can run back to the elevator, ride it down, then run back along the initial walkway, using the green crates as cover. However, this method is dangerous, and difficult to accomplish without suffering severe damage.

TIP

You can slide back to the first tower, then down to the security-building roof to drop Grenades and fight. Or, head back down the elevator, running through the crates on the walkway, and battling back to the helipad. Either way, you need that Armor on the side of the helipad opposite the security room.

On the helipad, mop up the last of the guards, head to the hatchway, and activate the switch to unlock it. Clamber down the steps, tag the guard if you haven't already, and head for the door at the end of the lower covered walkway section. Now comes the hard part–save eight world leaders!

Malprave Central Command-Dusk

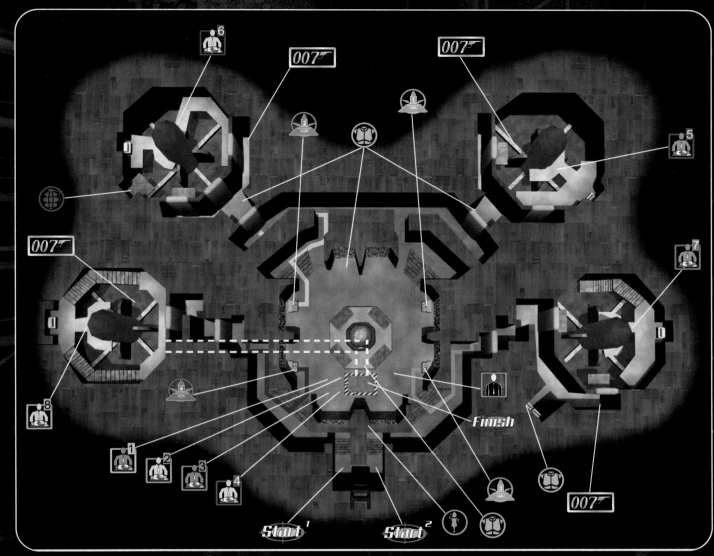

Start 1

Start 2

Finish

LEGEND

 Start - Start

 - Armor

 007 - 007 Bonus

 - Frag Grenades

 - Malprave

 - World Leader 1

 - World Leader 2

 - World Leader 3

 - World Leader 4

 - World Leader 5

 - World Leader 6

 - World Leader 7

 - World Leader 8

 - Silo 1 Door-Open Program

 - Silo 2 Door-Open Program

 - Silo 3 Door-Open Program

 - Silo 4 Door-Open Program

Finish - Finish

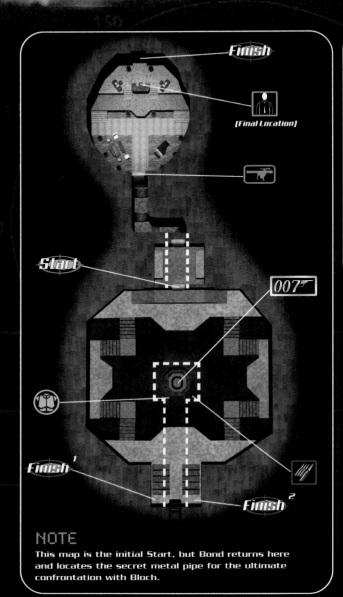

Finish

[Final Location]

Start

007

Finish [1]

Finish [2]

NOTE
This map is the initial Start, but Bond returns here and locates the secret metal pipe for the ultimate confrontation with Bloch.

LEGEND

Start	- Start
	- Armor
007	- 007 Bonus
	- Sniper Rifle Ammo
	- MRL-22 Rocket Launcher
	- Nigel Bloch
Finish	- Finish

Either stand on your balcony, aim with the telescopic D-17, and tag two or more enemies before the rest are aware of your presence, or continue around the platform until the enemy detects you (after you climb one set of steps). Then it's all-out

combat—aim down, taking out all four henchmen. You can even leap over the balcony, onto the floor, and chase down any guards trying to escape!

Once M has chimed in with some advice, open the door in front of you and peer over the balcony. It's the central intelligence operations room for Malprave's empire! This is a square room with four ground exits, a balcony around the top, and a high platform leading to the top of a huge holoprojector.

Your final choice is to ignore the shouting, run either left or right along the balcony, then out the exit on the opposite wall. This leads to a ladder and two passages—one left, one right. This is where the remaining troops are charging in. Attack!

If you ran into melee combat rather than sniping from above, the final enemy is in the central area, guarding four of the world leaders. Charge in and rattle off D-17 rounds (be sure not to shoot the world leaders!), then collect his PS100 ammunition. Four world leaders are safe.

Now to find the other four leaders. Refuel your Q-Jet from one of the compressed-gas canisters around the edge of the chamber, then hurry to locate the red computer station. This has the access code to infiltrate the first of the four silos joined to this room.

BEING BOND

While avoiding the guards, head up the catwalk ladder, run out onto the upper platform, and collect the Sniper Rifle ammo and another piece of Armor. Locate your Q-Laser, and zap the cabling in the center of this balcony. This sends the holoprojector crashing down into the central area, dispatching any guards standing underneath. Nice work, 007!

You can also zap the holoprojector cable from the side platforms to the left and right of the entrance to this room. Move slightly to one side so you don't hit one of the four support struts, and let the holoprojector fall! They can bill you later. Don't fall into the fiery crater the holoprojector left behind—there's no getting out of there alive!

TIP

Fill your Q-Jet tank before entering each silo area—you never know when you might need the Q-Jet!

Use the Q-Remote to unlock the door, then follow the red line left, around the corner, and up a passage to the right. Use the Q-Remote to open the blast door to silo 1. Step inside, grab the suit of Armor, and then head left to the opening to the silo.

The French leader is being held just on the other side of that gigantic Missile! The easiest way to rescue him is to look right and up at the Q-Claw mesh over the raised loading platform. Q-Claw over there, land on the platform, turn around, and immediately encounter both guards!

CAUTION

Take precautions not to accidentally gun down the world leaders. The game is over if any are shot by you or the enemy.

From your Q-Claw vantage point, jump down to the balcony the enemy was patrolling, and leave the French PM to escape. You need some weapons before you escape. Head back to the central chamber.

Wondering why R supplied you with a pair of Q-Glasses? To see through walls, of course! In silos 2 and 3, you can locate the guards by staring through the gray panels with the Q-Glasses on. This way, you can spot the enemies before they spot you.

When you enter the chamber, turn slightly right and run down to the second control panel. It corresponds to the yellow silo—number 2. Gather the information from the control panel. Then, with Q-Remote in hand, turn right, head up the three steps, turn right again, then turn left to the second blast door. Open it.

Tag the middle guard. As the other two react, swing left slightly and take out the guard by the control panel. This leaves one frantic guard to dispatch. He's likely to be running around near the two barrels next to the sealed exit.

The German chancellor's life is at stake in this silo! Head down the steps, then switch to your Sniper Rifle, and aim at the enemies ahead. There's one by the control panel, and one to either side of the missile. The chancellor is directly behind the missile.

A final guard appears out of a small chamber to the left of the control panel. Take this guard down from the central entrance, or from the balcony near the chancellor after you move through the hole in the exit wall. Leap from the control panel to the alcove, and collect three Grenades. If you fall into the silo, look up and Q-Claw to the entrance platform. Then exit to the central chamber—there are two silos to go.

Now for Silo 3. Start by running to the console diagonal from the area you just entered, and learn the code to open the green blast door. Then head left around the corner, following the green path, open the door, and jog around the winding corridor until you reach the window on your left.

The British prime minister is in danger! Walk around the interior passage, don your Q-Glasses to locate the enemy, and grab any Armor you need. Then return to the open doorway with the platform jutting out. Step onto the platform, and be warned: If you don't quickly shoot the guard nearest the console, he'll attempt to assassinate the world leader!

There are three ways to complete this silo. We'll cover the easiest way first. From the platform, either Q-Jetting down to the silo floor, or step left or right down to the lower platforms, then onto the silo floor.

Now at the silo floor, locate the door to the missile ladder, and Q-Laser the lock. Then climb up the ladder,

exit onto the balcony (the prime minister is directly to your right–watch that shooting!), and dispatch the guard nearest the console. Then fire at the remaining guards near the PM. Excellent work!

Your second option consists of dropping from the initial entry platform to the platform on your left. *Step*, don't jump, or you'll miss the lower platform and end up on the floor. Then look up and left to the Q-Claw mesh partly covered by an overhang. Q-Claw to it.

Once on the platform, quickly run up to close quarters, target the enemy by the console, then finish his chums without hitting the PM. You can also Q-Claw to the covered mesh area from the initial platform, although that is difficult to accomplish.

BEING BOND

Any leap down or to different platforms can be avoided by Q-Jetting to the destination instead.

The most complex route is to step off the initial platform to your right, before Q-Clawing to the mesh above the moving platform. Time your landing so you drop onto the platform rather than plummeting to the silo floor. Then, jump off the moving platform, grab the ladder, and then climb onto the balcony where the guards wait.

The U.S. president is in this silo! Tag the guard you can see, and then run left up the balcony until you spot the president. He breaks into a run, trying to escape the enemies. In the ensuing fracas, ignore the president, and concentrate on the guards, taking each down before they harm the president.

After you rescue the British prime minister, locate the doorway where you came in—it has a Q-Claw mesh above it, and is the easiest way to exit this silo.

The president has fled the area, and the door closes behind him, leaving you little choice but to descend to an open door at the bottom of silo 4. The easiest way down is via the Missile ladder scaffold, but a jump also does the trick. Follow the passage down, then right to Armor and an elevator.

One silo to go. Step to the blue silo, produce your Q-Remote, and activate the code. Run to the blue blast door by following the blue line along the ground, and enter. You see a circular path around the entire silo, and a guard to the left of the missile.

As you ascend into the main control chamber, Malprave appears. She's cheerful despite your sabotage, due to Nigel Bloch's arrival—he was sent to kill you. Again. It turns out you've been battling Bloch *clones* in past fights. This time though, it's the real deal—Bloch on a jetpack in a fight to the death!

TIP

Did you fill up on Q-Jet gas? You'll be thankful you did!

If you didn't destroy the holoprojector earlier, Bloch does so now. This means you must *not* fall into the central part of the chamber–even the Q-Jet won't save you from a fiery demise. Time to face Bloch's Rocket Launcher.

A better plan is to Q-Jet up to the second-floor balcony, and pick off Bloch while he's on the ground. You can step back and let the balcony floor absorb the Rocket strikes. Keep aiming and firing at Bloch until he flies up to the balcony.

Arm yourself with the D-17, and *keep moving*! Those Rockets hurt a lot more than anything before. If you're hit twice and you're still alive, locate the Armor in the cases on the exterior walls.

Bloch continues to fire, jetting to different areas of the balcony. Keep your distance, firing D-17 rounds until you run out, then switch to the PS100. When you see a Rocket, sidestep immediately, run a couple of yards, then regroup and re-aim. After being hit a number of times, Bloch leaps to the third floor.

Start by firing back at Bloch–whittling down his energy is the only way to win. If he runs, chase him, firing continuously. If he turns and fires, sidestep to a support strut, then run back. You can also circle-strafe around Bloch to dodge his Rocket attacks.

Bloch disappears down a secret shaft at the top of the chamber. Before he leaves he sends a shot crashing into the upper catwalk, demolishing it. Drop down, refuel the Q-Jet if you wish, then locate the circular exit. Above it is a Q-Claw mesh. To get a clear shot at the Q-Claw texture, Q-Jet onto the fallen walkway and climb up it to get a better angle. Activate the claw, ride it up to the circular entrance, and enter the blue passageway.

Defeating Nigel Bloch

After a short slide, Bond appears in Malprave's central office, where you previously met Bella and Bebe. This hall is disintegrating, and a wounded Bloch has dropped his Launcher and is hovering at the far end of the room. Drop to the ground and pick up the Launcher.

A countdown from 10 begins! The entire base is set to self destruct! Walk toward Bloch, aim up at him, and fire. If you miss, try again!

The platform you're on is quickly retracting into the raised area ahead, where the desks are! Keep moving forward. Don't sidestep left or right, or you fall into an abyss below.

When you hit Bloch once with your Rocket launcher, he is blasted out of Malprave's stained glass window, and falls to a spectacular demise on the rocks. The base explodes as Bond leaps out of the broken window...and lands on Nightshade's Harrier! With Malprave thwarted (she perished in the base explosion), Bond and Nightshade fly off to safety.

Bond will return...

The Tenets of Multiplayer

A multiplayer game takes place in a small- to medium-sized environment, in which two to four players compete. There are two types of multiplayer competition: agent training, in which players compete against each other, and cooperative, in which players form teams to compete against each other.

Environments

All of the multiplayer levels are located in a remote region of Scotland that MI6 has taken over. There, MI6 has a secret facility for training elite agents. On the outside, the facility looks like a typical 13th-century fortress. However, on the inside, the area is a fully functioning training facility, with video screens showing satellite link-ups. There is even a second Q-Branch setup here. This underground facility is below Haverrock Castle.

Game Modes

Combat Training

In this mode, up to four players earn their stripes by trying to dispatch as many opponents as possible within a time or score limit (you decide which).

Anti-Terrorist Training

 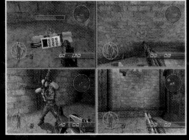

In this mode, two to four players try to defuse bombs to earn points. One bomb at a time is spawned into the level, and players must defuse as many bombs as possible. Points are also earned for dispatching the other players. To succeed, you must use the radar panel to navigate to the active bomb, and defuse it before engaging the enemy.

Bombs take a couple of seconds to defuse. If you want to ambush a foe, wait for an opponent to attempt to defuse the bomb, and then attack. However, more points are up for grabs when a bomb is removed from play, so learn the levels by play.

Top Agent

In this three- or four-player game mode, one player is the "Top Agent," and the remaining operatives attempt to dispatch him. The Top Agent has a different radar representation and looks different than the other players. To even things out, the Top Agent has a damage multiplier. In a three-player game, the Top Agent inflicts twice the damage that the other characters do, and in a four-player game, he inflicts three times the damage of the other players.

If the Top Agent is taken down, the executor becomes the Top Agent, and combat continues until the score or time limit is reached.

For best results, the other players should attack the Top Agent from opposite locations at the same time. The Top Agent should stalk enemies, closing in for the kill, setting traps, or locating cover to fire or snipe from. Players can only hurt their teammates if Friendly Fire is turned on.

Golden Gun (unlockable)

This game is for two to four players. One of the slots in the weapons list is the Golden Gun, which is a one-shot weapon with a reload time of about a second. The Golden Gun is one of the most deadly weapons in the game, easily discernable due to its color. Immediately locate and use it. For impressive results, fire at medium range after the gun has targeted, and keep a lookout for more ammunition.

Protect the Flag

 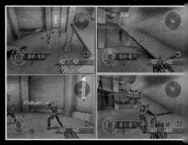

This is a two- to four-player game. When the game begins, a flag spawns at a predetermined point. Players rush to pick up the flag. The goal is to hold the flag for the time limit specified. If the flag carrier is killed, he drops the flag, and any other play

Flag timers are cumulative, so if you lose the flag, your counter doesn't reset. Points are awarded for takedowns and for keeping the flag until the countdown is completed. In team play, your team shares one flag timer, so your team must hold the flag for the total specified time.

Characters

First, choose one from 10 default and 6 unlockable characters. All of the characters work for Malprave, except Bond and his alter ego. Choosing a character is important—enemies clad in black, such as Stealth Bond, can blend into the shadows and hide with ease.

Bond

Malprave

Rig Diver

Super Thug

Bloch

Evil Zoe Clone

Griffin Clone

Jackal

Twin

Identicon Guard

Thug (unlockable)

Stealth Bond (unlockable)

Alpine Guard (unlockable)

Carrier Guard (unlockable)

Cyclops Oil Guard (unlockable)

Poseidon Guard (unlockable)

Weapons Detail

All of the weapons in the single player Bond experience are available in multiplayer. Please refer to "Inventory, Armory, and Vehicles" for advice on their uses. For tactics for using weapons in multiplayer training, please refer to the mission walkthroughs later in this section.

Some weapons are only available in multiplayer combat, including three types of mines. These weapons are detailed below.

Golden Gun

Starting Ammunition: 6 bullets
Chamber/Clip Size: 12/6 bullets
Rate of Fire: 1 round per second
Secondary Feature: None

Fire the Golden Gun once, and your enemy keels over. There's no measurable damage from this weapon–the enemy is either hit by it, or not.

Use the Golden Gun primarily from close- to mid-range (although far-range combat is possible). Wait for the auto-target to home in, then point and fire. Keep a steady arm, and make sure you have a clear shot; this weapon reloads slowly.

When you're defending against the Golden Gun, either charge headlong at the carrier, and hope he or she misses you (which is possible if you've already wounded the enemy), or collect all of the Golden Gun's limited ammunition (gold boxes of bullets).

Grenade Launcher

Starting Ammunition: 10
Chamber/Clip Size: 10/5
Rate of Fire: 0.78/2
Secondary Feature: Cluster Grenade

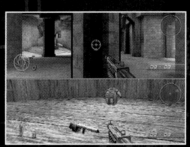

This Grenade Launcher is one of the most powerful weapons in the British military. The primary firing mode is to lob Grenades. The Grenades fire in an arc determined by the firing angle of the gun, just like in the single-player game. (The farther up you aim, the farther the Grenade travels, unless you're looking directly up. Then the Grenade drops back down near your feet.)

The secondary firing mode, the Cluster Grenade, doesn't explode, but rather shatters into six separate Grenades that explode, creating a massive blanket explosion. Switch between the two types of Grenades when you want to surprise an enemy who's chasing you, or when you want to cause a mass explosion at the feet of a charging foe.

If a cluster Grenade hits its target before hitting the ground, it explodes for an instant takedown. Stand where you can see all incoming enemies, and lob cluster Grenades a few feet in front of advancing enemies. When they get wise to this, let them chase you, then turn and lob Grenades as you run up steps.

Defending against a Grenade Launcher is difficult—we suggest running at your opponent with your Shotgun, or locating a Grenade Launcher yourself and returning the favor.

Photon Cannon (M16 Experimental)

Starting Ammunition: 5
Chamber/Clip Size: 5/1
Rate of Fire: 1.5 rounds per second
Secondary Fire: Blanket Fire

The Photon Cannon is the latest in a long line of the British military's attempts to create next-generation weapons. The primary firing mode launches a Photon Torpedo that homes in on the target and cuts it down, meaning you don't need an exact lock-on to fire—just pull the trigger while you're evading, and let the Torpedo do the rest. If it connects, expect an instant takedown.

However, if the enemy runs around a corner or by low archways or vertical beams, the Torpedo may miss. It may take three or four shots before you hit your target. Therefore, this weapon is best suited to wide-open areas.

To employ the secondary firing feature—hold the fire button for one second, and for each half second after that (while you're still holding it), the cannon builds energy. Release the fire button to fire one to five bolts. These are not homing Torpedoes, but they cause blanket eruptions that can down two enemies at once. The problem? Finding a wide enough area to fire it in. Narrow corridors aren't the best place to fire this from—you'll hit the walls.

Detonator Mines

These mines come with a Q-Remote. Place them on walls, ceilings, and floors. When placed, they sit dormant until the player triggers the Q-Remote, which detonates all of the mines. You can place a maximum of six Detonator Mines at a time. Place more than six, and the first one you placed detonates. You can

also detonate these mines by shooting them—an excellent tactic to use as an enemy passes a distant location. Detonator Mines are most useful when placed in a cluster on an inside corner so the enemy can't see it until it is too late.

Proximity Mines

You can place these mines on walls, ceilings, and floors. Internal sensors detect someone is nearby, then the mine detonates. You can place a maximum of six Proximity Mines at a time—place more than six, and the first one you placed detonates. You can also detonate Proximity Mines by shooting them. Place them in high-traffic areas, in dark spots out of view, and in areas where enemies like to hide. Just don't spend too long planting a mine—two seconds after placing it, it can explode and take you out if you're still nearby!

Trip Mines

Place Trip Mines on walls, ceilings, and floors. They emit a laser, which when broken, detonates the mine. You can place a maximum of six Trip Mines at a time—place more than six, and the first one you placed detonates. You can also shoot these mines to detonate them. Position Trip Mines around corners or in high-traffic areas to ensure detonation. Especially cunning agents will place these mines at the top of ladders.

Q-Gadgets
Q-Claw

More extensive information on the Q-Claw can be found in the "Q-Labs–Inventory, Armory, and Vehicles" section. Unlike the single-player Q-Claw, this device sticks to any surface, and can be retracted at any time.

This device allows you to cover large distances efficiently, climb to high alcoves and cover without Rocket-Jumping, or stick to sheer walls (if you keep the Gadget Activation button held). While hanging from a wall, rain fire on unsuspecting foes. Move from wall to wall to evade enemy fire.

Q-Jet

 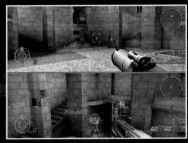

This device acts like the Q-Jet in the single-player missions, enabling short leaps upward for a couple of seconds. However, there is one important difference–this Q-Jet has limitless fuel. Each time you use the device, the fuel is used up as normal, but is replenished a couple of seconds later.

Power-Ups

These shields with "007" emblazoned on them give a temporary boost to the player that picks them up. All power-ups last 30 seconds, and respawn every 120 seconds.

Power

The player's damage is three times as powerful with this power-up. This one is amusing when used with the Grenade Launcher!

Shield

Players who have this power-up are three times as resistant to attack as normal players.

Healing

This power-up continually regenerates the player's Armor until it is fully recharged. The Armor is increased by 10 percent every half second. The Healing power-up does *not* directly heal a character.

Cloak

The player with this power-up becomes completely invisible. While the player is invisible he still casts a shadow, and firing weapons gives away the player's position.

Bionics

The player's speed is increased by 150 percent, including running and firing weapons. This power-up makes slower-firing ordnance more deadly.

Armor

The player that possesses this power-up is invulnerable to any form or attack. Players that have Armor are completely covered in metallic plating.

Boots (unlockable)

Players with Boots can jump many times higher than normal, and hang in the air as if they were in a low-gravity environment. Only the very skilled can master this power-up, because players hanging in midair are very vulnerable to attack. Try using a Rocket or a

Shotgun to hit someone while you're wearing the Boots. The enemy flies backwards!

Modifiers

Friendly Fire

Cooperative missions (such as Protect the Flag) take on a whole new meaning when the friendly fire affects you. Don't attempt lying in ambush on either side of a corridor with Grenades.

Full Arsenal (unlockable)

Players spawn in with all weapons in their inventory. This modifier promotes a higher level of game action, because players never need to spend time finding better weapons.

Golden Bullet

When this modifier is selected, the mission has no weapons or ammo pick-ups. All players spawn in with the Golden Gun, which has nearly infinite ammo, no auto-aim, and is a one-shot-kill weapon.

Low Gravity

The environment's gravity changes to low-gravity, allowing players to leap as if on the surface of the moon. Extremely entertaining, this sharpens your aiming skills to no end.

One Shot

All weapons used in the mission are *one-shot kill* weapons.

Persistent Weapons

A weapon is added to the players inventory, but stays on the ground. If the player already has that weapon, it won't be picked up. This modifier discourages players from camping (lying in wait) at a particular spot, and ensures that newly spawned players can pick up a weapon.

Random Weapons

Weapon pick-ups are replaced with boxes that give players random weapons. Players can only carry one weapon at a time. When you run over another, the contents of that box replaces your current weapon.

Safe Restart

This modifier forces players to spawn at the farthest location from all other players. This modifier all but prevents players from dying instantly. On the downside, it slows gameplay. This modifier is very useful on smaller maps.

Speed

Increase or decrease the players' speed to speed up or slow down gameplay. Slowing down allows snipers to practice their fire, while speeding up causes combat to be frantic.

No Falling Damage

When this modifier is set the player will incur no falling damage. This modifier is effectively used with rocket jumping and Q-clawing.

Teams

Players can choose from four different teams: Red, Blue, Green, and Gold. Once a player joins a team, the player's screen border and radar-blip are displayed in the team color. A targeted player's name is displayed in that player's team color.

By default, team members cannot damage one another. However, turning on the Friendly Fire option makes all players vulnerable. This can make for a more challenging and exciting form of team play. Teams can be composed of one to three players. You can play all game modes except Top Agent cooperatively. Each member of the team scores points, and those points make up the team total. The Results screen offers a per-player breakdown of all scoring.

Multiplayer Tactics

Use these strategies to maximize your chance of victory.

Go for Your Guns

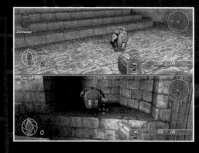

The first plan of action in any multiplayer game is to locate one or two suits of Armor. Attacking or defending without the benefit of Kevlar is foolish. Then, as soon as you find Armor, look for the most powerful weapon in the level. These are usually located on high or hard-to-access areas.

Snipe and Bomb

Before taking up roost in a high place (such as the roof of a building) to snipe at the enemy, collect both a Sniper Rifle and Grenades (either the Grenade Launcher or the FSU-4). This way, you can spend time aiming at enemies, and if they get to close, slip out of view, or attempt to charge, you can retaliate in two ways–with single-shot precision, or by covering a large area with minimal aiming.

Staying Serpentine

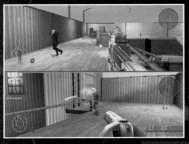 

The mark of a great multiplayer is the ability to wind through enemy fire without getting a scrape. First, you need to learn to sidestep out from cover and back again while keeping your target in the center of your screen. Then, if you want to charge an opponent or are evading a sniper, run in an unpredictable zigzag pattern. Make yourself difficult to hit.

Predicting Your Opponent

 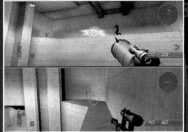

There's nothing more satisfying than landing a Grenade on an opponent 50 feet from your location with a single lob. Learning to fire at where your enemy *will be* and not where he *is* (primarily with projectile weapons), is a skill you must learn quickly. When you spot a foe running, launch a Rocket or Grenade at where your opponent will be when the ordnance connects; otherwise you'll be too late with your shots. This also works in close combat with Machine Guns–if your opponent is running down steps, wait until he rounds the corner, and start firing just before the enemy appears.

Setting Up Camp

Frowned on by many gamers, camping (staying in one secure place for long periods of time and tagging enemies from there) takes the fun out of multiplay. But if you're in this game to win, by all means claim a spot hidden from view (especially if you have the Cloak power-up), usually high up, and tag people with Grenades, sniper rounds, or Rockets. Move every so often to another spot. Ignore the whining of your fellow players–who said multiplayer was fair?

Screen Test

When two to three other people are all staring at the same game screen, any player can see where others are, stalling any ambushes or escape plans. Before a firefight, check the health and ammo of your intended victim–you can then calculate your chances in the combat zone. This isn't in the spirit of British manners, but there's a lot at stake here.

Hide and Seek

To keep people from finding your location, run to a safe spot or ambush point, and then look directly at the floor. With only cobblestones or metal sheeting to guide them, your opponents won't know where you are until it's too late. Don't spend the entire game looking at your feet, though–check your opponent's screen, and react to where they are.

Damage Control

Although there is a constant supply of Armor, there is no health available in multiplayer games, meaning you'll eventually fall to your opponent. If you're too proud to give even one point to your opponent, you might consider in-game suicide—if you're badly damaged, simply launch a Rocket at your feet. You lose a point, and start again with partial health, ready to take down the enemy.

Guard Duty

He who grabs the large weapon usually wins. Grenade Launchers, Rocket Launchers, Sniper Rifles, and other highly damaging weapons are hotspots for incoming enemies. If you patrol these areas, securing them so only you have access to the best weapons, you gain an excellent advantage. If you're the only player with Rockets, you have a greater chance of demolishing your foes.

Backing Up

It takes a couple of days of constant play to fully learn the layouts of the 12 multiplayer levels. Try running through entire levels backward. Why? It aids your maneuvering capabilities, and allows you to gun down enemies who think they're chasing you. If you can back up into Armor or a more powerful weapon while shooting at a charging opponent, you'll be unstoppable!

Easy Pickings

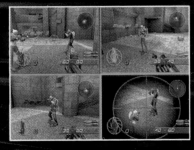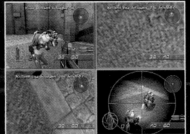

The last plan of multiplayer action is the most cunning of all, although it only works when you're playing against two or three opponents. While two of your enemies are engaged in a fierce battle, stay nearby, but out of sight. Just before one of them falls, wade in with weapons blazing, and take out both of the wounded players. That's two frags for the ammo expenditure of one!

Bots

The Nintendo GameCube and Microsoft Xbox consoles have an added gameplay bonus for fans of multiplayer—the inclusion of Bots. This bonus does not appear in the PlayStation 2 version. Bots are computer-controlled opponents that react like humans. The British Secret Service uses them to bring operatives up to speed. The following information describes customizing Bots, details the multiplayer maps featuring Bots, and offers tactics to defeat them.

Bot Benefits

Playing against Bots has several benefits over playing against human opponents. You can set their threat level and practice your own multiplayer tactics without revealing your strategies to other human players. Finally, all multiplayer maps are presented on a single screen when playing against Bots, making it a lot easier to see the levels in their entirety.

Bot Availability

Bots are available in two of the four multiplayer game modes: Combat Training and Top Agent. They are not available when playing Protect the Flag or Anti-Terrorist Training.

You can play against Bots in 10 of the 12 multiplayer maps: Dungeon, Town, Wine Cellar, Red Sector, Castle, Cooling Station, Abbey, Arsenal, Harbor, and Blue Sector. You cannot play against Bots in Escort, or the secret Rocket Arena.

Bot Options

Once you have selected your Time Limit, Point Limit, Map Settings, and Combat Training Map, press the Action button to bring up your agent-specific information. Move your cursor to the very bottom of your character's information area and select "Bots."

NOTE

More than one player can fight Bots in multiplayer games. However, the maximum number of players (both human or Bots) cannot exceed four. If you are playing on your own, you can choose between one and three Bots. If you are playing with a friend, the maximum goes down to two. With three, it is one, and with four human players, Bots cannot be selected.

Once you reach the Bot screen, choose between one and three Bots. Each Bot has individual options. This lets you create Bots of varying intelligence and cunning.

Inside the Bot Options screen, select the Bot's skill level. The three options are Easy, Medium, or Hard. Easy Bots tend to miss and stay in the open, Medium Bots have acquired rudimentary cunning and are great adversaries, and Hard Bots hardly ever miss and are difficult to beat. The default setting is "Medium."

Now select the team that each Bot represents, from Green, Blue, Red, or Gold. The default setting is that each player (human and Bot) is independent, although you can team up with one or more Bots to take on one or more other Bots in a team deathmatch.

Team deathmatches are great fun, especially if your Bot is "Hard" and aggressive! Stick by your Bot companion. Not only will you learn all their Bot tricks (such as where they like to hide), but you can provide covering fire, too!

You also can set up double ambush points inside levels, with your companion on one side of a doorway, and you on another. If friendly fire is off, you can attack enemies walking into your zone from both sides, giving them little chance to react!

Aggression ranges from Low to Medium to High, with Medium being the default setting. Enemies on Low aggression tend to stay back, evaluating combat, shooting from range, or waiting for an enemy to ambush. High aggression enemies swarm at you immediately with guns blazing and little regard for their own safety. Medium aggression enemies are in between.

Finally, choose a character model for each Bot. Remember that models with darker coloration, such as Bloch, are more difficult to spot in the shadows, and this does make a difference in combat.

The Top Agent option lets you play a multiplayer Bot match with slightly different rules, but the strategies learned from the level tactics still apply.

Bot Tactics

Although some level-specific tactics work better when playing against Bots, the previous strategies offered all work well.

Of course, lacking human foibles, Bots do have some advantages and disadvantages. They rarely make mistakes. They don't accidentally fall off ledges, and they always know where they are going.

Do you know all your exits? Can they all be defended so you're not overrun? If so, then this is a great spot to take out Bots from, as long as you can hide from their gunfire as well!

However, Bots tend to keep firing at one target until it is dispatched. This means Bots are easy to defeat when they're engaged in combat and you sneak up from behind. You usually can score a kill without a Bot turning from a firefight and hitting you.

Different strategies work depending on the number of Bots you select. Choosing only one adversary makes for a more tense deathmatch, but you can camp in one position and repeatedly guard the most powerful weapon.

Bots also follow the first person they see, unless you come too close. Use this to your advantage—stalk a Bot as it fires on another Bot, and once both enemies are wounded, step in and finish the job!

Finally, try playing the levels with different options, weapons, and power-up items for interesting and entertaining results. For example, don't expect victory if you select "Golden Gun" and set your three Bots' difficulty to "Hard!"

Bots however, are determined to strike you down. They always hit you when they spot you (and on Hard difficulty, this cuts you down in seconds as every shot hits). If you're caught in a firefight, be ready to receive ordnance continuously if Bots attack from behind.

The Dungeon

This uppermost level is a terrible place to stand but a great place to guard—beware of starting points near here. Bag the FSU-4 and run to cover. From here, step out into the open to lob grenades, or strike a Bot down one of the perimeter corridors.

Wait in an area containing a large and powerful weapon, and attack anyone venturing in to take it.

The two exterior corridors are deadly. Check your map—Bots almost always wait at one end of the corridor. If you're already in the corridor, they appear at one end to take you down. You can use this tactic too.

Wading into combat is advisable when playing against Bots only if you're not being tailed. Otherwise take up a strategic position in an easily defended area.

Bots also congregate at the bottom arena area with the Armor, and they fire at you from either side. They also use the cover provided by the mid-level raised area when you attack them from higher ground. Lob grenades in here for excellent results.

The best place to stay, as usual, is the raised area with the Windsor FSU-4. You can plug away at enemies near and far, and it's relatively straightforward to guard. Bot foes usually stop halfway up the steps to gain cover—grenades put a stop to that.

Town

Bots congregate in the center of town for a vicious (and usually rocket-based) firefight. Target this area for sniping, but never walk through unless the coast is clear—you could be attacked on multiple sides!

Bots are less likely than human foes to crush you as you descend into the main central wooden area to grab the Grenade Launcher. Or remain at the crushing lever and spin it when the Bots descend, as they often do.

The enclosed area with the sniper rifle, boxes, and shadowy tunnel is a great place to ambush or snipe from, especially with a power-up selected. However, this is also a spawning ground for incoming Bots, and an attacker is always nearby. Bots also like to ambush you from one of the narrow side streets—be wary!

Red Sector

It's difficult to actually make it to the middle of this level, thanks to the constant barrage of grenades and missiles. Bots here attack the first enemy they see, so sneak up and finish off those already engaged in combat.

The final area by the UGW, ramp, and Armor is a great place to stay and repel all Bots! Bots also hide at the bottom of the ramp and ambush enemies coming from the cobblestone street. Be ready to attack to the left and right, guarding the Armor. Or use the alcove to pick off enemies coming down the central street and from the fountain.

Possible "camping" sites for Bots include the underground tunnel area and one of the many balconies above the main area. Take an elevator up here, and use the cover afforded to rain grenades or missiles down on the Bots below.

Wine Cellar

As all players begin the match with the shotgun, keep close combat to a minimum, and dodging moves, such as leaping and running, to a maximum. The columned area can be a frantic place to stay, so keep one eye on the radar and the

Bots sometimes fire a couple of missiles at you, and if they miss, they often run to another location for a second try. Use the arena with the ramp to engage Bots in combat, perhaps staying underneath the balcony for cover. Bots also like ambushing you from a wall near the Rocket Launcher pick-up spot.

Castle

When you're running around the upper corridors of this level, expect to be shot at from the ground below or from gaps in the columns. This is more dangerous with Bots about!

Lob grenades at Bots fighting each other. Precise timing is required, but Bots tend to be more accurate with bullet-based weapons, so bring out your grenades.

Don't stand in the central courtyard long. Bots can hit you here and from cubby-holes up above. However, you're likely to find a new target in this area, searching for the Rocket Launcher. If you can't find an enemy, look down!

Cooling Station

Most of the firefighting occurs in the base lower arena; wade in and mop up a fight. The bal-conies sometimes hold a Bot, so approach from the upper level if you can.

Bots have an annoying habit of blasting you with precise and accurate shots as soon as you step through one of the many doors to the connecting corri-dors. Be extremely careful entering if your radar shows a Bot waiting.

Bots have trouble aiming at yo through stairs or at the bottor of steep angles, so attack fror above, using the balcony by your feet as a defense. Once you have the enemy on the ropes, leap down and finish th job. Try laying mines on a blinc corner for more exploding fun!

Abbey

You'll have most luck gunning down your opponents in the interconnecting corridors, especially if you attack from the tops of the sloping ramps. Use your radar to gauge where your foes are, and step to them, firing madly! The stone walls and many corners afford you cover and ambush points.

Bots usually end up in the crypt area with the broken ground above. There's always a firefigh here. If you can't find Bots, look here. But be wary of ambushes

Keep out of the expansive courtyards unless you must dash across, as the Bots hit you more easily here. Run across when the coast is clear, then attack your enemy from a corridor above. Spend only the time needed to pick up a weapon, choose an enemy, and begin the hunt!

Arsenal 20

Bots sometimes have a little di ficulty climbing stairs, so a grea ambush point is underneath a balcony, waiting at the end of one of the two blue pipe tun-nels. Shoot the Bot as it tries t escape up the ladder for a kill

Most of the action takes place at the central grilled platform. The area with the steam pipe and that interlocking corridor is a good place to stay, but keep moving!

To confuse your enemy, go high and tackle Bots from the upper balcony. Back up when you're under fire and use the floor for cover. Make sure your exits are well defended.

Harbor

Pick off Bots from the central lower wooden bridges with the Grenade Launcher. But be prepared to be peppered when you venture down. Don't linger here.

Hide in one of the two huts; Bots sometimes use these as ambush points. Then, when Bots are incoming, open the door, fire on them, and close the door again or step to the side into cover.

The UGW and sniper rifle are great once you become proficient. But remember that with the sniper rifle you'll get only one or two shots before a Bot retaliates! Hide behind boxes or on top of the building for extra cover; but beware—Bots are merciless, and the sniper rifle is difficult to aim. The preferred weapon is the UGW because it has a faster rate of fire.

Blue Sector

Find Bots in the lowest part of the level in the arena leading to the orange-lit tunnel. Step into this area once a fight is already under way for a couple of quick kills without too much retribution!

The right-angle corners dotted throughout the level make Bot ambushes almost a certainty, so be very careful and check your map before venturing into each room. You can ambush Bots yourself, but remember—hiding in the shadows makes you harder to hit, but it's also harder to escape if you're enclosed.

Bots tend to spawn, locate an enemy nearby, and then run after it shooting. Use this to your advantage—run to a recently spawned Bot, follow it as it attacks, and shoot it.

Missions

The remainder of this multiplayer debriefing runs you through some of the best positions, areas of interest, and other pertinent information. While this information is directed to those engaged in 00 Training multiplayer games, the majority of the tactics work on the other difficulty settings.

Dungeon

Location: Haverrock Ruins
Size: Small
Game Modes: Combat Training, Anti-Terrorist Training, Golden Gun, Protect the Flag, Top Agent
Default Weapon Set

Slot	Weapon
Slot 1	Wolfram P2K
Slot 2	Windsor FSU-4
Slot 3	Koffler & Stock KS7
Slot 4	Frinesi Special 12 Shotgun
Slot 5	Koffler & Stock D-17
Slot 6	Empty

Default Power-Up: Power
Number of Players: 2-4
Difficulty Level: Beginner

Check behind the broken brickwork to find a couple of barrels packed with explosives—shoot the barrels once with any weapon, and the wall section immediately to the right of it blows out. Don't worry—the falling bricks won't hurt you, even if you're standing on top of them.

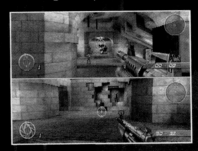

From here, you can storm in and grab that heavy suit of Armor, and then retreat outside. If the enemy catches you, it's very easy to become trapped in this area, so immediately head for more open spaces. However, if you weren't seen, this makes a reasonable sniping spot.

You can grab a more impressive power-up on the lowest level, near the vertical support struts. Simply aim and fire at the loose stone switch (shown in the screenshot), and the iron grating opens. Move in and out quickly; the grate descends soon. If you're stuck, aim and fire at the stone again.

Deep below MI6's Scottish hideaway lies a large dungeon with support struts, steps, and two hidden chambers. Start your multiplayer battles by familiarizing yourself with this introductory level; it's small enough for dramatic firefights, yet large enough for sneaky strategy.

The first of these hidden chambers is a piece of broken masonry along one of the exterior walls. It houses an important item. From the middle of the level looking down, turn right 90 degrees to spot it—it's on the second tier.

The many struts and curved corners make ambushing easy and reliable. Try fixing mines to the interior walls so they explode as an enemy rounds the corner, or stay on the bottom level in a

darker corner near the central steps and leap out to attack when a foe wanders in. There is Armor here–another reason to guard the area on the bottom level, near the central steps.

Go to the top level. You have a commanding view of the entire zone. Quickly check the map to learn where the enemy is. The FSU-4 (the most versatile weapon on this level) allows you to lob Grenades or fire all the way to the lower levels. Aiming down and firing is easier than looking up and doing so (you're more aware of the ground, and able to dodge).

Town

Location: Blackshaw Merse
Size: Medium
Game Modes: Combat Training, Anti-Terrorist
Training, Golden Gun, Protect the Flag, Top Agent
Default Weapon Set

Slot	Weapon
Slot 1	Wolfram P2K
Slot 2	Koffler & Stock KS7
Slot 3	MRL-22 Rocket Launcher
Slot 4	SSR 4000
Slot 5	UGW
Slot 6	Photon Cannon

Default Power-Up: Cloak
Number of Players: 2-4
Difficulty Level: Beginner

Blackshaw Merse is a settlement taken over by the British Ministry of Defense, and used extensively to train troops for urban warfare. The local inhabitants have been relocated, and the main village square turned into a training ground. A large arena to one side, a couple of smaller open areas, and a ramped road make sniping and ambushes excellent choices in this area.

Usually, enemies are spawned in the town square. From there it is only a short jog to the T-junction. Locate this area immediately, and guard it once you have the Rocket Launcher. Use the Launcher's secondary fire function to fire around corners and moving enemies. You can cause massive devastation with this weapon. Grab it!

The other area of interest in this area (aside from the Armor on the steps near the fountain, and the fountain itself, which is the best source of cover in this open area) is the dark alcove behind the pile of crates near the motorway signs. Here you have a commanding view of the dip in the road, and a clear path from the Rocket Launcher into the fountain arena. Set up with the Sniper Rifle in this area for excellent results, particularly in three and four-player modes, moving behind the boxes for cover.

The area to the left of the sloping road is a great hiding spot. Pick up the Sniper Rifle, the power-up, and more ammunition, then patrol the zone. The number of cross streets may appear to be high, but its really only two paths intersecting. This means that you can hide from the approaching Rocket, sidestep out from cover to fire, then step back.

This area also leads to another cunning hiding spot–the boxes at the end of the path near the dipped road lead to a ladder, which leads to a rooftop above the alcove where you found Armor. Here, you can use the

Sniper Rifle or Rocket Launcher, although you can't see people coming from the left. Stay here until you're spotted, then drop down—there's not much room to move out of the way of an incoming Rocket. Note that you can climb onto the sloped roof and continue left.

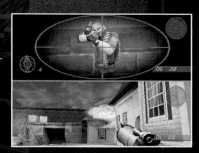

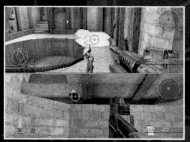

The Blackshaw Merse Abbey, an ancient ruined monastery, has many secrets, including a large wine cellar—a secret chamber deep beneath the Abbey. In the Wine Cellar, you'll discover the joys of Grenade-Launcher combat for the first time. Again, two main courtyard areas are connected by two corridor areas and a central trap, where you must recover the Grenade Launcher with skill and timing.

The road dips down to an area where you find Armor near the ramp up to ground level. In this area, you are susceptible to attacks from higher ground, and the best way to go from one area of the map to the other is via the narrow path in the middle of the map. Spend as little time here as possible, unless you're waiting at the main corner of the road to ambush an enemy.

The pillared courtyard houses Armor and the PS100—perhaps the most impressive Machine Gun in the game. Combat here could involve either this weapon or the Shotgun, and the pillars allow you step into cover while circling around your enemy. This is also an area to patrol, guarding the PS100 and watching for enemy incursions from the three exits.

Finally, the area diagonal from the main fountain courtyard, (where the UGW is) is another good sniping location. The higher ground is advantageous. From the small nook nearby, you can be view the entire middle corridor, allowing you to guard it. From there, it's only a small sidestep right to a view down the road and up to the houses and the other Sniper Rifle. Stay in this area and let the enemy come to you.

The opposite area is a wide open, raised courtyard—by far the best place to stand in this level. You can almost instantly spot incoming enemies, the area is deep enough to allow you to retreat backwards and not be caught in gunfire, there's Armor just down the steps, and if you're armed with the Grenade Launcher, you can lob Grenades. There are even extra Grenades near the left-hand steps in the central arena! Stay here and guard the Grenade Launcher.

Wine Cellar

Location: Haverrock Ruins
Size: Small
Game Modes: Combat Training, Anti-Terrorist Training, Golden Gun, Protect the Flag, Top Agent
Default Weapon Set

Slot 1	Frinesi Special 12 Shotgun
Slot 2	PS100
Slot 3	Windsor FSU-4
Slot 4	Grenade Launcher
Slot 5	Ingalls Type 20 Machine Gun
Slot 6	UGW

Default Modifier: Healing
Number of Players: 2-4
Difficulty Level: Beginner to Intermediate

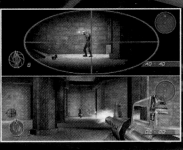

Your character can die in seconds in the middle arena, but the prize is worth it–a Grenade Launcher is up for grabs here! Drop into the large wooden cask, grab the Grenade Launcher and extra Armor, then climb the ladder and escape before an enemy starts the crushing mechanism. The two metal wheels (one on each courtyard) start the crushing. Also watch out when walking around the side of the cask–even a glancing blow from the crushing mechanism takes you out. If you see a foe in the cask, crush him as he climbs the steps. If the enemy is at the top of the cask, he drops the Grenade Launcher, which you can claim without risk.

Lob Grenades in high arcs from the open courtyard to hit every enemy you see coming. Alternatively, if stealth is your style, grab the UGW and prowl the pillared courtyard, hiding and tagging those ascending to this area. Finally, try running at an enemy with the Shotgun blazing–enemies armed with projectiles can't respond as fast as fast as you can shoot. This is the only effective way to remove a Grenade lobber from a courtyard (aside from using Grenades yourself.

Orange Sector

Location: MI6 Training Area
Size: Medium
Game Modes: Combat Training, Anti-Terrorist Training, Golden Gun, Protect the Flag, Top Agent
Default Weapon Set

Slot 1	Koffler & Stock KS7
Slot 2	MRL-22 Rocket Launcher
Slot 3	KA-57
Slot 4	Koffler & Stock D-17
Slot 5	Windsor FSU-4
Slot 6	Grenade Launcher

Default Power-Up: Cloak
Number of Players: 2-4
Difficulty Level: Beginner to Intermediate

The next areas of note are the two branching passages that lead from the pillared courtyard near the Armor, down steps, to a side entrance to the central chamber. Here you find two passages–one with a power-up and ammunition, the other with a UGW and a spike trap. Coax a chasing enemy in here and finish him with Grenades in this cramped space, or try sneaking to one of the courtyards using this route.

The orange color of this area's walls was designed to instill anger and hostile responses from those engaged in combat. The majority of the fighting takes place in a giant linked arena with a covered middle arch and two walkways around the top. At one end, a conveyor belt snakes around to a smaller arena and another platform corridor. This is the first opportunity to use the Q-Claw–make the most of it.

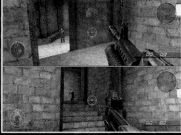

The other connecting passage at the opposite end of the map links the area where you find the PS100 to the Armor area before you ascend the steps to the open courtyard. The top of the steps in the pillared courtyard is a great ambush spot, as is hiding against the wall near the Armor, waiting for a foe to drop down, and then taking them down from behind.

The main area of combat in this zone is the giant arena. Start by finding the most powerful weapon (usually the Rocket Launcher in the middle). Firing at a foe from either side of the arena through the arch enables

u to select the Launcher's sec-
dary fire, and prevents your
pponent from hitting you. You
n also use the underside of
e ramp in this area to hide the
cket Launcher, taking out ene-
ies that come from the convey-
r or any of the other entrances.

lso of note is the balcony surrounding the arenas. Once you've
astered the Q-Claw, you can scoot up here without running up
e ramp. The balcony also provides a great place to stand and
re at those running below you. On the other side of the arch-
ay, the balcony continues around to a meshed floor–you can
e hit through this, so be careful. Finally, remember the eleva-
r that can deposit you either back on the ground or on the
alcony–although the Q-Claw makes this necessary only for
oaxing an enemy into a trap.

Q-Clawing is a joy–you can even clamp yourself to the ledge
bove the middle arch, and hang there waiting for an opponent
o run under you, then drop Grenades, fire Rockets, or use
Machine Gun fire. Also use Q-Claws to scoot up to the balcony
hat runs around this level. The balcony linking both
renas holds Armor, making a quick rappel upwards a great
means of escape.

Ground combat in the arenas is as fraught as it is frantic. Using
an Assault Rifle up close works just as well as a Rocket Launcher
if your opponent can't fire Rockets where you're running. Stay on
the periphery of the arenas so you always have an escape
route–standing in the middle of either arena is courting disaster.

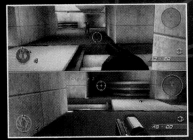

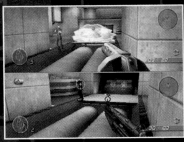

There's also a side arena that houses the Grenade Launcher
and ammunition, and is a great back entrance to the main
room. Standing and watching either entrance allows you to lob
Grenades or fire homing Rockets around walls. The balcony
above is a great place to ambush or take a breather.

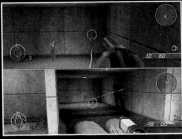

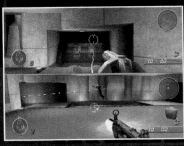

Finally, utilize the conveyor belt system in this zone, even though
the corridor is narrow and can be a deathtrap if numerous
Grenades are lobbed in. Q-Claw along the conveyor instead of
running to reach the corner, where there's a power-up. There's
another at the far end in the main area. Use this as an escape
route, or to sneak around from the large or small arena and
quickly attack.

Castle

Location: Haverrock Ruins
Size: Medium
**Game Modes: Combat Training, Anti-Terrorist
Training, Golden Gun, Protect the Flag, Top Agent**
Default Weapon Set

Slot 1	Wolfram P2K
Slot 2	UGW
Slot 3	Windsor FSU-4
Slot 4	MRL-22 Rocket Launcher
Slot 5	PS100
Slot 6	Grenade Launcher

Default Power-Up: Shield
Number of Players: 2–4
Difficulty Level: Advanced

This formidable castle is
shaped like a shield with tall
towers on every corner, and a
moat surrounding it, and it saw
no conqueror until King
Edward's siege in 1300.

As part of the MI6 Training Area, the castle ruins are used for agent training. The tall open structure is ideal for learning Q-Jet maneuvers and advanced weaponry. Although it's a narrow level, its height makes jetting of paramount importance.

Head around the balcony, using cover if you encounter an enemy (you can always escape onto the courtyard), and collect items. Wait for your opponent to drop into the courtyard, then take him out from higher ground. The stone walls act as cover.

Starting in the lower level of the grassy arena, this is the place for a power-up, and some fancy flying courtesy of the Q-Jet. Practice your leaps here, both around the courtyard, and up into the circular balcony running all the way around the level.

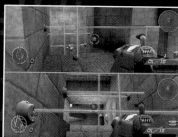

Try lying in wait at the top of the highest steps in the ruined alcove with the suit of Armor. In fact, any location with a commanding view of the level allows you to watch your enemies, and then strike when they are vulnerable. Getting as high up as you can enables you to see more of the level, and your victims have to strain their necks to find you. Just plan an escape route before you camp.

Combat usually takes place in the middle of the level. Remember that you now have an additional escape route–upwards, thanks to the Q-Jet. Utilize this ability if the situation looks grim. Also, aim down at opponents as you jump to tag them while they try to aim at you.

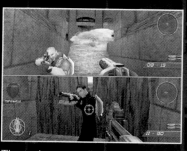

The stone walls and the narrow corridors between them are perfect for laying mines. Choose corners, high-traffic areas, and the tops of stairs.

Cooling Station

Location: Campbell Industrial Park
Size: Large
Game Modes: Combat Training, Anti-Terrorist Training, Golden Gun, Protect the Flag, Top Agent
Default Weapon Set

Slot 1	Wolfram P2K
Slot 2	Koffler & Stock K57
Slot 3	Windsor FSU-4
Slot 4	Koffler & Stock D-17
Slot 5	UGW
Slot 6	Trip Mines

There is a small entrance corridor leading to the locked castle gate. This is a good place to take a breather, but it's a dead end–the circular shape of the level means that most of the hiding takes place in the multi-level balcony overlooking the center. The steps leading to the balcony (not often used thanks to the Q-Jet leaping) can also be a great place to hide.

Default Power-Up: Strength
Number of Players: 2-4
Difficulty Level: Advanced

Choose the central area for most of your fighting. There are abundant items and weapons on the balcony and the floor, health, and a total of eight exits to use if combat isn't going your way.

Located in the southern sector of Campbell Industrial Park, the Cooling Station provides an intense, multi-level training experience for advanced recruits. In disrepair since its post-WWII decommissioning, and no longer cooling the adjacent power plant, the British Secret Service acquired this facility in 1978. Although water still runs through the pipes, it is only to establish the deafening and often confusing industrial atmosphere that agents in the field face everyday. Trainees have to master aerial assaults, Trip Mine placement and avoidance, and the prospect of taking fire from any angle.

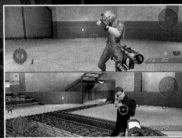

However, you don't want to wait in this area; the numerous exits mean you may be compromised by an enemy incursion at any moment. Also try shooting down from the balcony for easy hits, retreating when the enemy spots you.

This zone features doors that open, allowing you to wait and listen for the enemy. Stand in a corridor when you know an enemy is approaching, wait for the door to open, and fire–you have the advantage of surprise, and you can cut down a foe in moments.

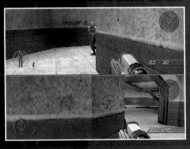

The corridors are a good place to ambush using Machine Guns or Assault Rifles. The corridors are narrow, sometimes feature blind corners, and can be confusing for your opponent if he is running and gets lost. Wait in the corridors until a door opens, and then pounce.

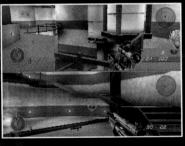

Although the level looks vast, it is only three chambers. There's an initial area in the middle, joined by four corridors. Two corridors lead to one chamber, and two to another of the same size. There's a second floor that has balconies instead of rooms. Once you realize this and can recognize which room is which (one side room has an elevator, the other a spiral staircase), finding your way around becomes much easier.

One of the two side rooms has an elevator. Use it–there's Armor and a power-up on the balcony it leads to. Otherwise, prowling this zone isn't a good plan. The bottom floor is recessed, allowing an enemy to charge in from the corridors and target you–there's only one cooling pipe to hide behind! Stay on the top floor of this chamber.

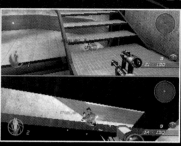

The other room doesn't feature quite as impressive a balcony as the first (there's only one suit of Armor to take), but the ground floor has a dark area where you can ambush enemies—especially those walking down the stairs. The flat floor in this area makes exiting a little easier.

Abbey

Location: Haverrock Ruins
Size: Medium
Game Modes: Combat Training, Anti-Terrorist Training, Golden Gun, Protect the Flag, Top Agent
Default Weapon Set

Slot 1	Wolfram P2K
Slot 2	PS100
Slot 3	Photon Cannon
Slot 4	KA-57
Slot 5	Grenade Launcher
Slot 6	Proximity Mines

Default Power-Up: Bionics
Number of Players: 2-4
Difficulty Level: Intermediate

What was once a proud medieval monastery is now a ghost of its former self. The Abbey ruins are now home to combat veterans intent on utilizing their skills in arena combat and perfecting fighting in narrow, high corridors. The Abbey is two huge chambers with exits along one wall, and a small maze of interlocking corridors with one chamber overlooking a basement area.

The initial chamber on the slightly lower level is large, and has two entrances leading up to the corridor area on one side, an exit from the lower level, and a corridor around the back of the main area. Combat in such a wide open space requires some special ordnance such as a rapid-fire Machine Gun or well-aimed Rocket. Shotguns at midrange just won't cut it, so run toward enemies here—there's plenty of room to show off your strafing and dodging techniques.

Moving up into the criss-cross of corridors, ramps lead to another large arena-like room, but the corridors themselves are where you can have some fun, even with the weapon you enter the game with the Shotgun. Close-range Shotgun and Machine Gun fire is best, because Rockets are a little difficult to fire on the move. The many walls provide hiding places and cover.

The second arena is similar in size to the other first one, aside from the gaping hole in the middle. The hole allows you to peer into the basement of the Abbey, and aim at the enemies in there. Simply step back if they start firing, and watch for foes charging into the arena from the corridor entrances.

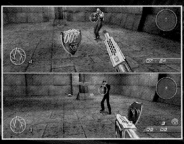

Drop into the basement, where a number of choice items are available, including the power-up. Spend a bit of time in the basement, or perhaps use the exterior walls as cover—wait for an opponent to jump down from the ramp, and then attack. You can also guard the end of the initial arena from one end of the basement, and stand on the ramp to launch a surprise attack on enemies charging down the ramp. All in all, the basement is a reasonable spot to stay.

The only way out of the basement is a long narrow corridor that leads to the initial main arena. A narrow wall leads to a suit of Armor, but watch out—you can be attacked from above, from the arena, and even by enemies following you out of the basement!

Stepping out from the basement to the arena usually results in an attack. It's difficult to dodge until you enter the arena, and the narrow dead-end corridor can be a death trap.

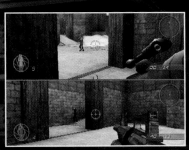

If you want an alternative route from the arena to the corridor complex, head for the exit in the initial arena on the exterior wall. This leads up and around a corner, and ends at the highest point in the level. This is great for sneaking up on enemies, and the view from the gap overlooking the basement exit and arena is perfect to stage an ambush.

Arsenal

Location: Campbell Industrial Park
Size: Large
Game Modes: Combat Training, Anti-Terrorist Training, Golden Gun, Protect the Flag, Top Agent
Default Weapon Set
    Slot 1   Defender Pistol
    Slot 2   Trip Mines
    Slot 3   Frinesi Special 12 Shotgun
    Slot 4   PS100
    Slot 5   UGW
    Slot 6   Koffler & Stock D-17
Default Power-Up: Healing
Number of Players: 2-4
Difficulty Level: Intermediate to Advanced

Only a few miles from the Cooling Station, the Arsenal is the staple of MI6 explosives training. Originally a small munitions plant used toward the end of WWII, this semi-subterranean industrial building, with its tight hallways, provides realistic combat encounters in which both conventional small arms and experimental explosives play a decisive role. Agents must learn to both avoid and utilize the pressurized steam pipes throughout the Arsenal.

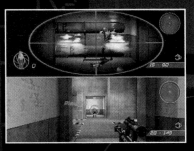

There's more to firing at pipes than meets the eye. When you're standing on the middle section, on top of the area with the two blue tunnels, shoot the pipes at the end. Steam escapes, and continues to do so throughout the game. If you hear steam escaping, but you're not in that area, you know that another player has entered the steam area.

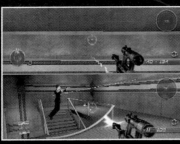

Never use ladders in this level–they are difficult to climb off of. Instead, employ the Q-Claw to ascend and descend–the central area and the steps up to the top balcony are perfect for the Q-Claw. Take care firing the claw and becoming stuck halfway through a maneuver.

Drop from the "+"-shaped platform, and you discover mines, Armor, and great weapons in the blue pipe section beneath. There are two exits–a short tunnel leading to another balconied area away from the main action, and a curved pipe leading to steps and an entrance leading back to the central area. Both areas are great for waiting for enemies to emerge from the tunnels, but watch your step as you do so. The power-up and items in this lower level are worth the risk.

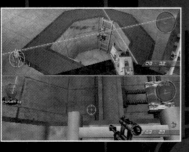

This is an excellent level on which to use mines–learn where your opponents emerge or drop from, and then place a mine there. The tops of ladders, on the floor around corners, and on the floor at the top of steps are effective places to plant mines.

The area adjacent to the pipes–a storeroom with many boxes–is a great place to fight with Machine Guns or Shotguns, and the crates provide excellent cover. Hide behind crates, wait for your victim to run past, then chase him down, firing as you go. Remember, the smaller room and the exit to the stairwell are useful hiding spots as well.

The final areas of note are the balconies. A staircase leads to a winding balcony ending in another set of stairs, and the top of those stairs is an excellent place to stand and fire. Then there's the semi-circular balcony, reached by ladder, the Q-Claw, and a leap from the central area. This is a low-traffic zone where you can look down and fire without being attacked from all angles.

Harbor

Location: Blackshaw Merse
Size: Large
Game Modes: Combat Training, Anti-Terrorist Training, Golden Gun, Protect the Flag, Top Agent
Default Weapon Set
> Slot 1 Koffler & Stock KS7
> Slot 2 Detonator Mines
> Slot 3 PS100
> Slot 4 SSR 4000
> Slot 5 UGW
> Slot 6 Grenade Launcher

Default Power-Ups: Power
Number of Players: 2-4
Difficulty Level: Intermediate to Advanced

Located close to the town of Blackshaw Merse, the Harbor area has long been closed to fishing boats, and even the Coast Guard is not allowed near—live weapons training is continuous in this zone. Three buildings (two of them close together), a crisscross of wooden planks, and a square balcony provide ample space to hide, charge, attack, and snipe. In fact, this is a sniper's paradise, with three Sniper Rifles available.

The building to one side of the interlocking passages and the other buildings is important. Open the doors in the building to get from one raised balcony to another without walking the planks below, and find the rather PS100 in the building itself. Go up either of the ladder entrances to the roof, which holds a Sniper Rifle and two boxes of ammo. Climb here with Grenades as backup, and move slowly, targeting enemies below. You're sure to rack up the points.

Diagonally across from the solitary building are two more buildings. The farthest one has a ladder leading to the underside of the main balcony—a great place to escape to and from. Head out of the door toward the first building, then immediately go left to find another Sniper Rifle and another ladder. The ladder leads to a slanted roof with less room to move, but is more

The final building features three exits—the upper exit leads up a ramp to the second building, the middle exit allows you to mount a charge up the ladder of the solitary building, and the third exit is lower (at sea level), and provides quick and covered escape from the planks below. Find the FSU-4 in the building. This is a good place to pass through and has many ambush points, but too many exits to be safe.

The smaller of the two balconies runs from the second building (and the second Sniper Rifle), across the side of the third building, and then leads down to the solitary building. You have a commanding view of the area from this balcony (of course, you're also prone to attack), and this zone is great for lobbing Grenades or running into any of the buildings. Near the Sniper Rifle is a dark alcove at the back of the exterior ramp to the third building. There's Armor there. Only grab the Armor when you're not being followed—there's little room to move.

The other balcony is U-shaped, and runs all the way around the perimeter of the level from the second building to the solitary one, with two ramps down to the planks, a number of boxes to hide behind, and a ladder in the far corner leading down to a third Sniper Rifle. The exposed nature of the balcony means you should quickly run to better cover, or take cover behind the boxes. However, if the enemy is in the planked area below, use this balcony to attack from or use it as a jump-off point to a lower level.

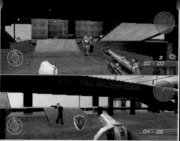

Now comes the area at sea level. This huge planked section houses a power-up under the bridge (you can wade in water, but it slows you down terribly). On top of the bridge lies the Grenade Launcher, in the most open area of the map. It's worth grabbing the Launcher though, because it can fire to almost any open area on the stage. You can get anywhere you want in this area—there are numerous exits, and even a far corner to snipe from. And if the sniper is bothering you from atop the building, grab the Grenade Launcher, run to the side of the building, and lob Grenades at him.

Blue Sector

Location: M16 Training Area
Size: Medium
Game Modes: Combat Training, Anti-Terrorist Training, Golden Gun, Protect the Flag, Top Agent
Default Weapon Set

Slot 1	Defender	
Slot 2	PS100	
Slot 3	MRL-22 Rocket Launcher	
Slot 4	UGW	
Slot 5	KA-57	
Slot 6	Grenade Launcher	

Default Power-Up: Bionics
Number of Players: 2-4
Difficulty Level: Advanced

There are too many excellent places to hide and fire from on this level to detail here, but we'll provide tips for each room, starting at the end room. This is an excellent area in which to wait for combat. There are three exits—the left and middle ones (via the balcony), both leading to the central arena, and the right exit heads down into an orange tunnel area. Under the ramp to the balcony is a great spot to ambush from.

The orange tunnel area isn't the best place to run down, because enemies have an advantage if they're on higher ground. Fortunately, there's a power-up and Rocket Launcher here, and the narrow walls make Machine Gun combat an excellent choice. From the initial room, head down to a doorway in the left wall leading to the central zone. There's another exit at the far end.

ne of the most impressive feats of British engi- eering, this combat zone has multiple levels, any corridors, and a couple of large arenas ith many hiding places—however, the complex is uch smaller than it appears, thanks to crafty chitecture. This facility is used as the train- g area for using the Q-Claw.

The multi-level central area is the place for combat and hiding. From the balcony in the initial chamber, there's Armor, and then a narrow stone foundation on the right leading to a power-up—Q-Claw your way there. Then, Q-Claw up to the opposite corner, and lob Grenades or Rockets on enemies below. With five exits, all roads lead here. Just don't spend too much time at the bottom of the arena—you're an easy target.

When you reach the central chamber from the balcony leading from the initial room, turn left and head down the corridor. This is one of the many doorways to this arena. Turn right to enter a second mini-arena with many more places to stand and fight. This area doesn't have the Rocket Launcher like the main area does, but the FSU-4 is an excellent second choice. You can even Q-Claw up above the doorway on the right and hang there–one of many places for an ambush.

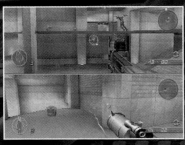

Take either the lower corner exit or the balcony doorway opposite. After a short corridor romp, you enter the final chamber, with another five exits to choose from! This is why it is easy to get lost in this environment. One exit leads to the orange tunnel, three head back to the previous chamber, and one heads back to the central arena.

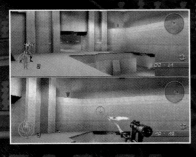

Always take time to head for the central arena–it contains the best weapons, plus there are three suits of Armor nearby. When you get tired of Q-Clawing up ramps and zipping around learning the level, visit the ultimate sniper location–the lights on top of the central arena! Hold your Q-Claw in place and aim at anyone that enters this domain.

Train Station

Location: Blackshaw Merse
Size: Small
Game Mode: Combat Training
Default Weapon Set

Slot 1	SSR 4000
Slot 2	Empty
Slot 3	Empty
Slot 4	Empty
Slot 5	Empty
Slot 6	Empty

Number of Players: 2-4
Default Power-Ups: Armor
Difficulty Level: Intermediate

Train passengers usually don't venture into the wilds of Scotland, and they especially avoid the train station at Blackshaw Merse–partly because the surrounding area is off limits to the public, but mainly because the station has been turned into a sniper's playground. There are two opposing station buildings with a platform in the middle, and many places to hide and plug from long distance. Your goal is to either guard or take down a VIP, depending upon the whim of those controlling the death match.

The roof is by far the best place to be on this level. The roof provides enough room to move and tag an opponent anywhere on the level. The extra elevation means opponents on the ground find it difficult to see you, but you must aim and fire at foes on the opposite roof before they spot you. Stay on the roof, changing position every once in a while, and use the chimneys as cover.

Move down into the interior of the building (which is identical on each side). There are numerous windows to peep through along the main corridor, which also features stairs leading to the roof. Be forewarned however, that a rooftop sniper has the advantage over a recently respawned player in this area, because it is difficult to look up and locate snipers. Use the walls as cover if you're being fired on, and rush up the steps without pausing.

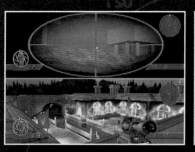

The short corridor at the front of each building is another good sniping spot. Thanks to the windows overlooking the side and the front of the platform, you can tag the VIP moments after the train leaves. The extra width of this area makes it easier to avoid sniper fire. Take care, though–snipers can hit you through the walls.

You earn extra points for taking down the VIP and the picking up his briefcase. When he exits the train, one sniper must protect, while the other must try to dispatch the VIP (he's carrying a suitcase). You are also sometimes charged with taking out both the VIP and the other sniper. Simply aim from the area that juts out from the roof on the right, aim down onto the platform, and fire.

The train platform isn't the wisest place to be. There's a sniper on the opposite building, so you're a sitting duck without the cover the station provides. The alcove in one corner is a good place to hide, and the back entrance to the interior of the station is a great place to duck back into. However, the platform is the easiest place to stand and take down the VIP, but standing around is suicide. Seek cover at once!

Rocket Arena (unlockable)

Location: MI6 Training Area
Size: Small
Game Mode: Combat Training
Default Weapon Set
Slot 1	MRL-22 Rocket Launcher
Slot 2	Empty
Slot 3	Empty
Slot 4	Empty
Slot 5	Empty
Slot 6	Empty

Number of Players: 2-4
Default Power-Up: Bionics
Difficulty Level: Advanced

When the train pulls away from the station, find the steps down to the track (diagonal from the station entrance) and quickly step down. Grab the ammunition pick-up, and then go up the opposite steps. If you're too slow, the train will hit you.

The ultra-secret Rocket Arena, the basis for MI6's continuing training in low gravity fighting, is not available to all operatives. You must meet certain mission parameters before the British government will allow you access to this zone. Once you have access, you see that this is essentially one huge arena flanked by two large doorways on each side. There's also a raised tunnel entrance at each end. The entrances lead to a small underground tunnel; however, these are grated and can't be entered. Here, you learn to aim and fire projectiles in low gravity once this feature has been obtained. The following strategy should be used when fighting in low-gravity conditions.

The arena itself is immense—larger than any open area you've entered previously. The size enables you to target your enemy as you slowly leap through the air. As soon as you spot a foe on your radar, leap toward him, firing at where you think he'll be in a couple of seconds. Another approach is to leap to the side, then turn and aim as you move.

Don't look to the tunnel as an escape route—it's likely to be a deathtrap instead. Running down the ramp and into the central area does allow you to pick up the only power-up on the level, but it also lets your foe know where you are, and he'll be ready with a Rocket as you climb back up the ramp. Switch directions and return the way you came, spinning around a couple of times first so the enemy doesn't know which end you appear from. Jump out of the tunnel as soon as you can!

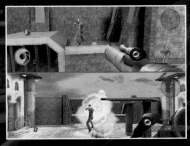

Judge where an enemy is likely to land, and have a Rocket detonating when the enemy gets there. You must jump, especially over the heads of your opponents, and then aim down and blast them.

In the exact center of the zone is a hole in the ground. If you drop through it, you land on top of a power-up. However, the dip before the hole makes lining up the drop problematic. The dip slows you down and allows the enemy more than enough time to tag you. Leave this hole alone—there are quicker and safer ways to enter the sublevel by running down the ramped areas.

The corners of the lower area and the tops of the doorways along the side of the arena are choice places to lie in wait. Until your opponent figures out where you are, you can leap up, spin around, crouch to make yourself smaller, and fire away.

Visit the two tunnel entrances at either side of the arena—there's a suit of Armor on the roof of each tunnel entrance. With the Armor, you can take a couple of extra splash damage hits, but nothing directly. Remain on the roof, especially if your opponent is close by and can't see you—then leap off the raised area, turning to fire at the enemy.

Secrets

Welcome to the Secrets section, where we reveal 007 Bonus Pick-up locations, along with the prizes up for grabs!

Gold Rewards

Should you complete a mission and score enough points, you are rewarded with a Gold Medal. This is more than just a shiny emblem–it unlocks a game secret designed to enhance your single-player experience. Each mission has a single Gold Medal that gives a particular reward, as follows:

Mission	Reward	Notes
Trouble In Paradise	Golden Gun	P2K replacement, ultra-powerful pistol
Precious Cargo	Golden CH-6	Rocket Launcher with ammunition
Dangerous Pursuit	Missiles	For use in Missions 3 and 7
Bad Diplomacy	Golden Accuracy	Upgrade for Golden Gun
Cold Reception	Golden Clip	Upgrade for Golden Gun
Night of the Jackal	Golden Bullets	Upgrade for Golden Gun
Streets of Bucharest	Lotus Esprit	New car for Missions 3 and 7
Fire & Water	Increased Fire Rate	Upgrade for Golden Gun
Forbidden Depths	Golden Armor	Double Armor capacity
Poseidon	Golden Grenades	Double-damage Grenades
Mediterranean Crisis	Regenerative Armor	Golden Armor regenerates
Evil Summit	Ammo	Upgrade for Golden Gun

NOTE

The unlocked reward is displayed on the Mission Select screen for the corresponding mission.

NOTE

Note that Golden Rewards are defaulted to "ON" when received, but you can turn them off in the Options Menu by selecting "Golden Rewards–OFF".

but with one important difference–it has mores ammunition; useful for obtaining all the 007 Bonus Pick-ups in this stage!

Reward Specifics

Golden Gun–Action Missions Only

The Golden Gun replaces the P2K in the player's inventory. Initially it delivers more damage, but its true value comes to bear when you get the "golden" updates.

Golden CH-6–Mission 2 (Precious Cargo) Only

Available from the beginning of the mission, this functions in the same way as a regulation CH-6 Rocket Launcher,

Unlimited Missiles–Driving Missions Only

All the fun of guided Missiles, without the pain of running out of them! Available from the start of either driving mission, this cuts out clever techniques from your foes, and allows mass destruction of both ground and airborne enemies!

Golden Accuracy–Action Missions Only

Tired of having your long-range shots spray all around their target, but never hit? This upgrade makes your Golden Gun 100 percent

go exactly where you point the weapon. Your Golden Gun becomes a sniper Pistol!

Golden Clip-Action Missions Only

Another upgrade to the Golden Gun, this doubles the capacity of each clip, allowing you to fire double the shots before reloading.

Golden Bullets-Action Missions Only

Yet another upgrade to the Golden Gun, this significantly increases the damage each shot does, making the gun much more powerful. Now this weapon is as effective as some high-powered Assault Rifles!

Lotus Esprit-Driving Missions Only

Take control of this premiere roadster that has exceptional speed and handling. A classic Bond car from the 1970s.

Increased Fire Rate-Action Missions Only

Another Golden Gun upgrade, this increases the rate of fire of the gun, turning your once-humble P2K into an even deadlier semi-automatic Pistol!

Golden Armor-All Missions

This turns the Armor HUD in the bottom-left corner of your screen gold, reducing the damage you take whenever you are hit.

Golden Grenades-Action Missions Only

This replaces the regulation Frag Grenades. Any Grenades you obtain now are gold. Each time you start a mission, you receive three Golden Grenades. They have the same large explosion radius (so be careful!), but will do more damage than regular Frag Grenades.

Regenerative Armor-All Missions

When your Armor is almost depleted and this reward is activated, your Armor recharges without the need for additional Armor. It can regenerate enough to charge from near death to about 33 percent of full Armor in around 30 seconds. Bang on!

Unlimited Ammunition-Action Missions Only

This is an upgrade for the Golden Gun only. You must still reload the Golden Gun, however.

007 Bonus

These golden, floating 007 logos are usually scattered in out-of-the-way places in every mission. They are available *only* after a player wins a Gold Medal in a level (at [00 Agent] difficulty). There are three to nine Bonuses per mission. When you find a Bonus, a sound lets you know you've added it to your collection. Collect all the Bonuses in a mission and score a Gold Medal rating to receive a Platinum Medal. (See the "Platinum Rewards" section further on.)

The Bonuses are shown on each map in the walkthrough. Additionally, we reveal each one's location in the following section.

007 Bonus Locations

Trouble In Paradise

Pick-up 1: Q-Claw to the top of the building; the Pick-up is just before the drop into the ventilation shaft.

Pick-up 2: In the security room at the bottom of the elevator, on top of a pile of crates.

Pick-up 3: Behind the third row of plants in the "lights out" room, to the left.

Pick-up 4: To the left of the metal walkway that leads to the view of the submarine.

Precious Cargo

Pick-up 1: Take out both vehicles at the roadblock before the alley (you automatically receive the Pick-up).

Pick-up 2: Shoot the helicopter that does a flyby at the park.

Pick-up 3: Shoot the foot soldier spying on you from down the street left of the park.

Pick-up 4: Kill all three guards at the gates to the factory.

Pick-up 5: Take out the henchman across from you in the central corridor of the factory by shooting the fan underneath him.

Pick-up 6: Blow up the tank in the factory and proceed without killing all of the henchmen.

Dangerous Pursuit

Pick-up 1: Behind the player's starting location at the dock.

Pick-up 2: Inside a crate near the exit from the dock—blow apart the crate, and the logo is inside.

Pick-up 3: In the middle passage of the convention center near the water.

Pick-up 4: Behind the gas station near the convention center.

Pick-up 5: Just around the corner from the subway entrance on the left side, where the trees start as you approach the west subway entrance.

Bad Diplomacy

Pick-up 1: In the back corner of the room at the end of the first-floor hallway.

Pick-up 2: In the secret room on the second floor, beyond the laser beams.

Pick-up 3: On the far side of the large, domed rotunda, second floor.

Pick-up 4: Behind the trophy cases on the third floor, past Griffin's quarters.

Cold Reception

Pick-up 1: In the "wrong door" room to the player's left at the start of the mission, where masses of guards appear if the wrong button is pushed.

Pick-up 2: In the second duct between the octagonal rooms.

Pick-up 3: Just to the right of the small staircase that leads into the mainframe room.

Pick-up 4: In the cavern, down the flight of stairs beside the steam canister.

Pick-up 5: In the second duct above the first cavern.

Pick-up 6: Behind a canister on the ground floor of the second cavern.

Pick-up 7: On top of a canister on the ground floor of the second cavern.

Night of the Jackal

Pick-up 1: On display in a store window, up the road beyond the first sniper.

Pick-up 2: Behind the second sniper near the safehouse.

Pick-up 3: Inside the Embassy, in the second office to the right after coming up the stairs.

Pick-up 4: Behind crates on the helipad.

Streets of Bucharest

First Section

Pick-up 1: Underneath the bridge.

Pick-up 2: In the shortcut at the top of the first hill (after retrieving Q-Locator).

Pick-up 3: At the far end of the train tracks at the station.

Pick-up 4: In the air after the second rooftop shortcut jump (after retrieving Q-Locator).

Second Section

Pick-up 5: Hit the oil tanker between the two vans shortly after you spot the helicopter hovering over the bridge; the logo appears at the end of the road.

Pick-up 6: Destroy both of the helicopters in front of the hotel; the logo appears in the hotel lobby.

Fire & Water

Pick-up 1: Behind barrels on the first rooftop by helipad 1, near the door you Q-Laser.

Pick-up 2: In the small room beyond the first grating you Q-Laser (the grating to the right).

Pick-up 3: Behind the first crane on the main deck near the two suspended crates.

Pick-up 4: Underneath the exit door on the main deck.

Pick-up 5: On the platform on the far side of the pump room.

Pick-up 6: On the upper deck outside above the pump room, to your right when you step through the door.

Pick-up 7: Between the two large canisters outside above the pump room.

Pick-up 8: Behind barrels in the middle tower room where you face the helicopter.

Forbidden Depths

Pick-up 1: Destroy all the gun turrets; the logo appears near the end of the maintenance tunnel.

Pick-up 2: Take out both of the guards in the first tower; the logo appears underneath them.

Pick-up 3: Take out both of the guards in the second tower; the logo appears underneath them.

Pick-up 4: Destroy all of the land mines; the logo appears at the end of the passage.

Poseidon

Pick-up 1: In a small duct in the first room.

Pick-up 2: Behind barrels in the entryway control room of the first large laboratory.

Pick-up 3: Behind the entrance stairway of the second large laboratory.

Pick-up 4: In the small storeroom in the submarine bay control room.

Pick-up 5: Around the corner behind the large crane, near the base of the far stairs to the ground floor of the sub bay.

Mediterranean Crisis

Pick-up 1: In Bond's cell.

Pick-up 2: At the far end of the first duct that leads out from the brig.

Pick-up 3: On the balcony outside, where Bond starts if he succeeded in the previous mission.

Pick-up 4: In the duct that exits the first control room in hangar 1.

Pick-up 5: Near barrels beside the second Harrier in hangar 2.

Pick-up 6: On the upper deck outside hangar 2.

Pick-up 7: Under the stairs beyond the conference room.

Pick-up 8: On the deck outside, overlooking the depth charge deck.

Pick-up 9: Behind the depth charges.

Evil Summit

Pick-up 1: Behind the top of tower 1.

Pick-up 2: Behind the top of tower 2.

Pick-up 3: On the catwalk above the large holoprojector in the central command room.

Pick-up 4: On the ground floor of silo 1.

Pick-up 5: At the far end of the hallway leading to silo 3.

Pick-up 6: Opposite the door on the ground floor of silo 4.

Platinum Rewards

You can earn a Platinum Medal by obtaining a Gold score and collecting all 007 Bonus Pick-ups. You claim extra multiplayer items each time you receive a Platinum Reward. The available rewards are as follows:

Mission	Reward	Type
Trouble in Paradise	Rocket Manor	Map
Precious Cargo	Golden Gun	Game mode and weapon
Dangerous Pursuit	Bond Combat	Character
Bad Diplomacy	Gravity Boots	Power-up
Cold Reception	New Thug type	Character
Night of the Jackal	Viper	Weapon
Streets of Bucharest	Alpine Guard	Character
Fire & Water	Calypso	Weapon
Forbidden Depths	Full Arsenal	Modifier
Poseidon	Cyclops Oil Guard	Character
Mediterranean Crisis	Poseidon Guard	Character
Evil Summit	Carrier Guard	Character

NOTE

The reward unlocked is displayed on the Platinum Medal reward screen, and is also displayed on the Mission Select screen for that mission.

PRIMAGAMES.COM

More Than Just Strategy

Strategy:

Over 250 Fast Track Guides with many more to come — new online strategy every week.

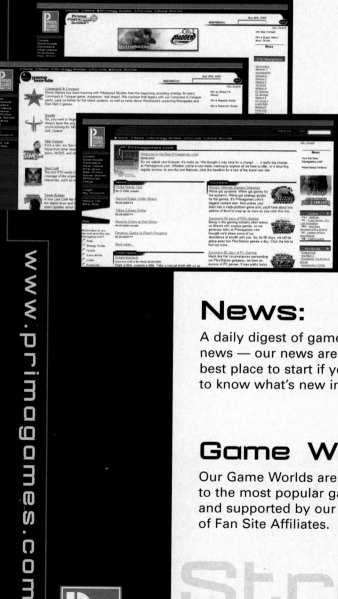

News:

A daily digest of game industry news — our news area is the best place to start if you want to know what's new in games.

Game Worlds:

Our Game Worlds are dedicated to the most popular games and supported by our wealth of Fan Site Affiliates.

PRIMA GAMES .COM

Home ● News ● Strategy

STRATEGY GUIDES

Fast Track Guides

Perfect Dark

Space Channel 5

Everquest

Syphon Filter 2

Tomb Raider

The Sims

Codes
Downloads
Contests
Interviews
Previews
Ask Prima
Game Saves
Affiliates
FAQs

Login
My Account

About Us
Site Map

www.primagames.com

PRIMA GAMES .COM®